School Projects in Natural History

School Projects in Natural History

Edited by
The Devon Trust for Nature Conservation

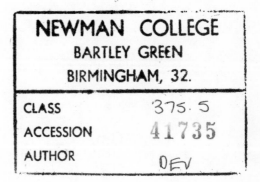

Heinemann Educational Books
London

Heinemann Educational Books

London Edinburgh Melbourne Toronto
Johannesburg Auckland Singapore Hong Kong
Kuala Lumpar Ibadan Nairobi New Delhi

ISBN 0 435 59920,8

© Devon Trust for Nature Conservation 1972

First published 1972

Published by Heinemann Educational Books Ltd
48 Charles Street, London W1X 8AH

Printed by photo-lithography and made in Great Britain at
the Pitman Press, Bath

Preface

The collection of this set of projects is the culmination of a process which began in 1964. A Plymouth teacher then proposed to the Devon Trust for Nature Conservation a scheme for the encouragement of individual and group field work in schools. The original scheme envisaged that the Trust should accept the results of natural history work undertaken by pupils in Devon, have this work commented upon and judged by experts in the relevant fields, and pass both comment and judgment back to the teacher. A Certificate of Merit would be presented to those achieving reasonable standards in this scheme.

After all schools in the County had been consulted about the scheme, it became clear that energy and enthusiasm were available, but knowledge of what to do and where to start were sometimes sadly lacking. The Trust could see that the first step should be to supply projects in Natural History for the schools.

Experts in various branches of natural history and practising teachers inside and outside the County were asked to contribute to a collection of project material. The first Project Book was published in duplicated form in June, 1965. The material offered had been sifted, edited and in some cases rewritten by a small committee consisting of I. S. Cummins, M. J. D'Oyly, L. A. J. Jackman, T. R. Jenkyn, I. D. Mercer, and R. J. Revell. Ken Watkins, who did most of the material collecting, convened their meetings and saw the book through the printer's hands. The first printing soon ran out. To the Trust's corporate surprise it sold to education authorities in this country and abroad as well as to schools and individuals. It was reprinted four times in the next three years. Immediately the search for more subjects was begun and in 1969 a second volume was produced.

Material for yet a third book was being amassed — geared to specific under-used habitats — when the opportunity to proffer the whole scheme to a wider audience occurred. The publishers wished to collect all that existed so far into one book — hence this volume.

The range of subjects is wide and the standard of learning required variable. It is hoped that there is something here for all levels of scholarship.

To facilitate selection by the teacher a simple code has been applied to the projects as follows:

S – simple;   **I** – intermediate;   **A** – advanced.

These three classes might be interpreted as roughly applying to primary schools, secondary schools to fifth year, and sixth forms respectively. However, many projects are capable of adaptation to all levels, and the compilers claim no superior ability in their classification. Each teacher should feel free to adapt and amplify as he or she thinks fit, and yet to the sixth-former one would still say sophistication is all around us in 1970, but there are a multitude of simple facts which are still unknown. Many a project here described for junior classes is no less a contribution to knowledge for all that — please do not reject simplicity.

This extension of the original scheme is offered now for its own sake. The submitting of results to the Trust for comment by experts is still a matter for the individual teacher or school and they are under no obligation to do so. For its part the Trust can take no responsibility for the activities of individuals or groups as the result of the production of this book except its moral responsibility with respect to the conservation principles to which it is dedicated. The Trust feels that the teacher using this book will implicitly share this responsibility at least to the extent of instilling the following code into his or her pupils before work commences:

A good student working in the countryside leaves as little trace as possible of his activities and causes the minimum of disturbance of the local inhabitants whether people or animals and plants. To this end he:

(i) does not collect animals and plants unless a small number of specimens is essential for accurate identification.

(ii) replaces immediately all stones, logs, etc., turned over during investigations and takes care to avoid trampling unnecessarily the vegetation under foot.

(iii) is careful to disturb as little as possible the animal-life of the countryside and, of course, never takes eggs from birds' nests.

(iv) always obtains the owner's permission to enter private property and, if necessary, special permission to collect there.

Those of us who teach and learn in the countryside are as much a part of the total pressure on it as the excavator, planter, or recreator. Above all, we should be the ones who recognize the risks. We should teach and learn about the care and management of the countryside so that those now learning shall have some to teach from, some to manage and a great deal to enjoy, and so that the opinion of all is brought to bear upon the decision-makers in this respect.

The Trust wishes you every success in your field work.

IAN MERCER

1972   THE DEVON TRUST FOR NATURE CONSERVATION

Contents

School Projects in Natural History

Birds

Insects and Spiders

Snails and Slugs

Trees, Woods, and Hedgerows

Plants other than Trees

Plants other than Trees (*continued*)

Ponds and Rivers

Seashore

Acknowledgements

Acknowledgements for permission to publish the photographs which appear in this book are due as follows:

Gordon Burgess, p. 37, 45.
Bruce Coleman Ltd., p. 150.
Forestry Commission, p. 111.
Leslie Jackman, p. 1, 161 and jacket photography
Natural History Photographic Agency, p. 71.
Ray Palmer, p. 9, 25, 43, 90, 154, 157, 165, 174.
K. Watkins, p. 23, 27, 32, 40, 66, 69, 72, 76, 84, 85, 93, 97, 100, 105, 108, 134, 141, 143, 144.

GENERAL

Project 1

The Integration of Natural History Projects into other School Work

by K. W. Dendle   [S]

This is an account of an experiment carried out with a class of nine- and ten-year old boys attending a school in an urban district. The aim was to enable the boys to make a practical study of natural history, and to integrate this study with other subjects on their timetable.

The site selected for study was a wood close to the school. The boys studied letter-writing in their English lesson, then wrote to the owner of the wood asking permission to carry out the study, and the best effort was selected and sent. The letter was sent in error to the owner's son, who entered into the spirit of the project and replied suggesting the rightful owner could be ascertained from the Ordnance Survey Numbers of the wood. This gave material for another lesson, and led to a visit to the Council Office where the appropriate sheets were inspected and the numbers obtained. The owner of the wood gave the boys *carte blanche*, and a letter of thanks was sent from the boys.

They made their equipment during the art and craft lesson. Collecting nets for insects and river work were made from wire, canes and old nylon stockings, and notepads were made from cardboard, wallpaper and plain paper. A screw-top jar was adapted to serve as a killing jar as follows. The bottom of the jar was covered with cotton wool, and a piece of wire gauze was inserted as a protective barrier. A layer of Plaster of Paris was poured into the gauze, and this was pierced several times with a needle before it hardened. One boy was made responsible for the jar when in use, and ethyl acetate was introduced as required under supervision. Any average-sized beetle or insect could be quickly put to sleep in this jar. Empty flat tins for transporting dead insects were lined with cotton wool, pieces of dowelling rod were measured off in metres and centi-metres for measuring plants or plumbing depths of water, and ropes were marked with twine at fifteen-centimetre intervals for measuring such things as the girth of a tree. Tins of plaster of Paris were prepared and plasticine put in polythene bags for leaf prints, and polythene bags were also obtained for the transportation of plants and river specimens.

Five groups of boys were formed for the study of birds, insects, flowers, trees and the river. Work sheets were prepared for the guidance of each group.

The visits started early in the summer term in time for the birds' nesting season. With children of this age, one could not expect a detailed study of individual items, and an overall picture was aimed at instead. This was made possible by introducing comparisons; quadrats, counts and findings from their own observations and knowledge were all of great use. For instance the beaks of the woodland birds were compared with those of the estuary birds, and this gave the boys an insight into evolution. From the quadrats they found that the plant life differed in various parts of the wood and surrounds. The influence of drainage, overhanging trees and animal life were accordingly introduced. The river group found counts very exciting; regrettably there was no pond at hand for a comparison. The groups with the greatest number of things to do were the most interested over a long period. The tree study included bark rubbings, leaf prints (Plaster of Paris with plasticine mould), lead prints with light sensitive paper, and this group's interest never waned; on the other hand once the nesting period was over and the fledglings flown, the bird study group found it difficult to sit bird watching, but interest was revived by introducing counts.

Work in school kept pace with the field work. The answers to questions on the work sheets were turned into accounts of the subjects studied, complete with the boys' own drawings. These were mounted on cover paper in the form of concertina type booklets, the covers being suitably designed during art lessons. A display was arranged and new items were constantly added. A photographic record was also kept, and mounted in an album made in school.

The project leant itself to a certain amount of correlation with other subjects. Discussions concerning the visits took up most of the Oral English time; the speed of the river was found; the number of trees estimated after a small area count had been taken; the time taken in getting to and from Tutshill was found; and of course the letters written.

Project 2

Detecting on the Way to School

by Phyllis Bond   [S]

This project can provide a great deal of interesting study for children who have a long walk to school and can make them use their opportunities. It is not suggested as a class project, but as a piece of work for those who find it suits them.

Look for traces of animals—hair and wool on wire; cones and nuts; owl pellets, etc.

Note birds seen and whether seen in same spot regularly.

Watch for migration, nests (even in winter when hedges are bare).

Study the plants through the year—keep a record of their appearance.

In *winter* note skeletons, derelict stalks, evergreens; study shapes of trees.

Spring — shows the struggle for light and air under the hedgerows. Note the areas rich in plant growth and compare with poorer areas. Watch tree buds.

Summer—notice climbers, make study of umbellifers, etc., seed dispersal, grasses.

Autumn—make collections of berries, seeds, fruits. Note appearances of trees, collect leaves.

Study the position of the sun through the year—note lengths of shadows.

Note the effect of frost and snow.

If a river or stream is passed, take note of its level and the effect of heavy rain.

Notice clouds and direction of wind.

Project 3

The Scope of Natural History Project Work

(NATURAL HISTORY PROJECTS FOR SCHOOLS IN THE MILTON KEYNES AREA)

by Max Hooper   [S—I]

Introduction

The Milton Keynes Research Committee was established in November 1967 to survey, investigate and recommend for preservation, sites of archaelogical, historic and natural history interest in the designated area of the new city of Milton Keynes.

At the first meeting it was noted that some sites could be used for long-term research projects to show the effects of the new city on wild-life and an Advisory Sub-Committee for Natural History was therefore set up to plan the necessary work.

At a meeting of this Sub-Committee it was suggested that a number of useful and interesting projects could be tackled by school children and a meeting, between teachers and members of the Natural History Sub-Committee, was held to discuss some of the problems. The outcome of the discussion was that some concrete suggestions for projects were drawn up by the Sub-Committee and circulated to schools to indicate the type of work required.

The Projects in General

The Sub-Committee felt that many projects to chart the changes caused by development could usefully be tackled by school children from the senior forms of primary schools to the sixth forms of secondary schools. Three general types of project are possible:

1. Presence records on particular species of plants and animals over a period of years.

2. Numerical data on populations over a period of years.

3. Records of habitats and their changes over a number of years.

All three types required an early start, standardization of recording, continuity of recording and a pooling of results. An early start was necessary if we were to achieve realistic base lines from which to measure changes. Standardization of recording was necessary to ensure comparability between results achieved by different schools, to facilitate analysis of the results and make continuity of recording easier. If for example one school works in an area which becomes designated for open air recreation and another school records in another area, initially similar to the first, which becomes an industrial site, it would be important to know what differences in the results were caused by differences in recording methods and what differences in the results were caused by the differences in development. Also if one school drops out after, say, two or three years of recording, it would be very much easier with standard recording methods for another school to take over.

This means that in the projects which follow there are some recording proformas which may at first sight appear rather formidable. They should prove to be relatively simple on closer acquaintance.

Group 1   Presence Data

The basic premise of this type of observation is that there are gross differences between species in their sensitivity to the projected development. Hence records of presence over the whole new city area made over a period of years should show changes in distribution and status of these more sensitive species. A species of bird, for example, may disappear entirely from the area.

Two types of recording are possible: first, regular recording in one specific area to which the school has access such as a grass field with hedgerows, a small copse, a stretch of stream or a green lane, and second, casual records of sightings made over the school catchment area by children as they travel to and from school.

Records of easily identified species only should be made as suggested on the proforma (Appendix 1) which should be suitable for 8–10 year olds recording a small paddock with a pond in it.

For casual sightings each species will require its own proforma examples (Appendix 2).

This type of recording has the serious fault, from the school's point of view, that changes may be slow, particularly in, say, the first five years of development, and therefore recording may not be continued year after year because changes are not apparent. The regular recording of these common species is, however, very important. Either the casual sighting records should be kept in conjunction with one of the more intensive studies or the records should be made in two ways. That is, one set of records could be made for school use in the form of a large scale map of the area, be it field or catchment area, on which coloured pins or the childrens own drawings of the animals could be put in the places where they were found for classroom display, and another set of formal records could be compiled from this for the central pool of records.

Group II   Numerical Data on Populations

The basic premise here is that some species may not be so grossly sensitive to the changes consequent upon development that they disappear entirely but that they will show some effects which can be measured by counting, or estimating by some standard method, the number of individuals in a given area each year.

The Numbers of Animals

An example of this type of project is the British Trust for Ornithology Common Bird Census, in which populations of nesting birds within an area are estimated from the numbers of male birds singing or other reproductive behaviour patterns such as defending a territory. Full details of this project are obtainable from the B.T.O., Beech Grove, Tring, Hertfordshire, but it cannot be unreservedly recommended to schools as considerable degree of expertise in recognizing species of birds is required. However some schools might well record the presence numbers and distribution of singing males of one or two readily recognizable species, such as blackbird or robin, within a limited area or in one specific length of hedge along somewhat similar lines to this survey.

Most other animal population counts depend upon some form of trapping or sampling and here a word of warning is necessary. It is possible even with the best line traps to damage the population under examination, and a teacher responsible for a class which would like to undertake this type of work should consult some competent authority for advice before beginning.

The basic method is to trap, mark and recapture a sample of the population; then if X animals are caught, marked and released and subsequently Y animals are caught of which Z are found to be marked, the total population will be $\dfrac{X \times Y}{Z}$.

A possible set of results might be:

No. caught, marked and released (X)	= 156
Total No. recaptured (Y)	= 200
No. of the recaptured animals which were marked (Z) =	15

Then the total population would be $\dfrac{X \times Y}{Z} = \dfrac{156 \times 200}{15} = 2080.$

In practice the trapping and marking methods and the interval between the two trapping times must be adapted to the animal under examination. For work to be repeated each year the season and the weather conditions over the period of sampling should be the same each year.

1. The size of an insect population in grassland
   (a) *Site:* The site should be open meadow, heath, rough grass, etc., free from trees or bushes or any very great irregularities in the vegetation. Preferably the area should be defined by hedges, ditches, walls, etc., to prevent undue immigration of the species. The vegetation should be described in general terms and an accurate grid reference given.
   (b) *The animal:* Froghoppers, grasshoppers or ladybird would be suitable.
   (c) *The apparatus:* Sweep nets, pooters, small tubes, ethyl acetate and a quick drying cellulose paint.
   (d) *The method:* Using the sweep nets capture about 200 animals. Mark them with a very small spot of the paint and let it dry taking care to keep the individuals apart so that legs are not stuck with the paint. If they are very active and difficult to mark use a whiff of the ethyl acetate to anaesthetize them, mark them and allow them to recover and dry off before releasing them. The marked individuals should be released at random throughout the sampling area. About four hours later the sampling area should be swept again until at least as many insects as were caught the

first time have been caught again. Count the number caught and the number of them that are marked and hence calculate the total population.

2. Woodlice in woodland
    (a) *Site:* The site could be any small copse or some reasonably limited part of some larger wood such as a glade. Again the vegetation should be described and an accurate grid reference given.
    (b) *The animal:* The woodlouse *Oniscus asellus* (Refer to Cloudsley-Thompson and Sankey, *Land Invertebrates*, published by Methuen, or Savory's *The world of small animals,* for pictures, descriptions and keys to prevent confusion).
    (c) *The apparatus:* Paint, if necessary, small tiles or pieces of broken asbestos sheeting.
    (d) *Method:* For 'traps' use stones, fallen logs, etc., which occur within the area. If these do not occur, put out the pieces of asbestos sheeting or tiles as traps. The day after the traps are put out collect and mark the woodlice that have collected under them; on the third day re-examine the traps and count the total number of lice and the number of marked animals and calculate the total population as before.

3. Earthworms in arable land
    (a) *Site:* Any tilled field or ley. A brief description of the area including the current crop and an accurate grid reference should be given.
    (b) *The animal:* Earthworms *Lumbricidae.* (Refer to Cloudsley-Thompson and Sankey *Land Invertebrates* for descriptions and diagrams of the common species).
    (c) *Apparatus:* Watering can, 8 litres water, 16 g potassium permanganate; stoppered vials of 4% formalin and quadrat frames.
    (d) *Method:* 8 quadrats of 0.25 m^2 area are placed at random within the field and these areas watered with potassium permanganate solution at the rate of 2 g permanganate per litre of water per square metre. The worms will come to the surface and should be collected quickly and placed in the vials of 4% formalin. They should be taken back to the school for identification and the calculation of the total population.

Note: These are just three projects: many others are possible using similar methods for different animals. The methods can be refined quite considerably and their use extended to such other features of populations as the age structure.

Numbers of Plant Populations

The numbers of plants within an area may be easier or more difficult to discover than the numbers of animals. Plants have the advantage that they do not move but it is often difficult to decide what constitutes an individual (several shoots may come from a single root). Also it is common to find that plants are not randomly or uniformly spread within an area so that sampling on a small scale will not give a true picture of a population. It is perfectly feasible in a number of cases to count individuals in quadrats of known area and hence estimate the population as was done for the worms, but more definite figures can be obtained by counting every individual in a circumscribed population. This is best done by mapping the occurrence of the individual plants.

4. The numbers of plants in a population
   (a) *Site:* Woodland with bluebells. Again a brief description of the site and an accurate grid reference are required.
   (b) *Plant:* The Bluebell. Other suitable plants would be cowslips, primrose, orchids, etc.
   (c) *Apparatus:* Two stout wooden pegs about 6 cm x 6 cm x 54 cm, two nails and two 15 m tape measures.
   (d) *Method:* The two pegs are driven into the ground until only about 12 cm sticks out, at a distance of about 415 m apart, adjacent to the population to be mapped. Each peg has a nail driven into the top surface to hitch the tape onto and one peg is marked A and the other B. The position of each plant can then be measured from these two fixed points and if required some additional data about each plant may be written down at the same time. Back in the classroom an accurate map may be drawn with a ruler and a pair of compasses and how well each plant is growing can be indicated, for example with blue pins for flowering, green pins for leaves only and red pins for plants that have been picked or damaged by trampling.

   If this type of recording were repeated each year an estimate of the effects of the impact of people picking wild flowers could be made.

Group III   Recording Habitats

So far we have been concerned with recording the presence of species of animals and plants in an area or estimating the numbers of a single species. Usually to record a habitat in a meaningful way one must not only record the presence of a representative range of species but also give some estimate of each one's performance. Hence to a greater knowledge of and ability to identify plants and animals must be added some sophistication of technique. On the other hand some important habitats may be defined and described using a limited number of plants

only. These include arable land, some cultivated grasslands (leys) and
hedgerows.

One of these habitats, the hedgerow, is already covered by a national
recording scheme, full details of which are given later (Appendix 4).
This scheme is not designed to monitor the more subtle changes which
might occur over a small area in a limited time but could be modified to
do so by the addition of some numerical index of the frequency of the
species in a 30 m length: for example by giving the percentage of the
30 m length made up of hawthorn, elder and blackthorn and by recording the same 30 m lengths year after year, i.e. using them as permanent
quadrats. If this were done, counts of nesting blackbirds, woodlice, etc.,
as described above might also be done at the same time. Similarly
quadrats might be set up within a grass field or wood and the performance of each species in them recorded each year. In the case of arable
fields and grass leys, however, the rapidity of change in flora with crops,
sprays, grazing and other management practices make it necessary to
use some other quadrat method. One possible method is frequency
analysis and a project on a grass field or area of heath is perfectly
feasible using this technique. In frequency analysis it is necessary to
record only the presence of a species in a large number of small quadrats
and the results are expressed as percentage frequency of occurrence:
if species (*a*) occurs in 25 out of 200 quadrats then its percentage
frequency is 12%. Naturally this method only gives realistic results if
all the plant species are uniformly distributed in the area sampled, the
quadrats are placed at random within the area, and the area itself only
contains one kind of plant community.

Frequency analysis of weeds in an arable field
(*a*) *Site:* Any arable or ley field preferably of small size (so that
adequate supervision can be given!). A description of the field,
its soil and crop and spraying regime plus an accurate grid
reference are necessary.
(*b*) *The plants:* Arable weeds. As a farmer is unlikely to allow
school children to roam in a standing crop it is probable that
access will be limited to times when the weeds are just seedlings.
Fortunately weeds are usually readily identifiable at this stage
with the *M.A.F.F. Bulletin* No. 179 'Seedlings of common weeds'
which has very clear diagrams and excellent keys and costs only
22½ p.
(*c*) *Apparatus:* Quadrat frames. These may be made of stout wire or
thin welding rod about 20 cm square.
(*d*) *Method:* Records from at least 100 quadrats may be necessary.
In some years less may be adequate to describe the weed flora
but it is better to use the same number each year and thus
maintain the same degree of accuracy.
These quadrats must be placed at random, A usual method is
to walk haphazardly through the field throwing the quadrat over

one's shoulder at intervals and recording the weeds where it falls.
If a rag is tied to the frame it is easier to find in denser vegetation.
The presence of species is then recorded as shown below on
squared paper (Appendix 5).

Final Words

1. Always obtain permission to enter private land and permission to
   do experiments or collect material.
2. Never collect plants and animals unless strictly necessary for the
   purpose of the experiment or for identification.
3. Never disturb animals or trample vegetation unnecessarily.
4. Remember that the owners of land on which you have worked
   might well like to know what you have achieved and as an act of
   courtesey your records should be made available to them if they
   wish it. At least the offer should be made.

Appendix 1   Presence Records for a Specified Site

Grid reference	Name of site
Date of record	Name of recorder
Description of area:	

Species seen	Comment
Blackbird Cuckoo Great tit Peewit Skylark Starling Wood pigeon Yellow hammer Fox Hare Hedgehog Mole Rabbit Squirrel etc.	

Note: on Presence Record Proforma I.

1. Species seen should be ticked in the column and any species which
   were not recorded for some reason, such as difficulty of identification
   of time of visit, should be noted.

2. The list of species may be as long or as short as individual schools or classes might think reasonable. For example, even for the younger classes insects such as earwig, daddylonglegs or woodlouse might be added, as could frogs, toads, newts, etc., where they might be expected.
3. Each visit must be recorded on a separate proforma.

Appendix 2   Records of Casual Sightings

In this case it will be best to keep a separate proforma for each species, e.g. for hares:

Hare records		Name of school		
Locality	Date	Comments	Name of observer	Grid reference

Appendix 3   Plant Mapping Record Sheet

Project: Bluebell mapping		
Locality:		Grid reference:
Date:		
Name of school:		
Description of area:		
Distance from A	Distance from B	Comments

Appendix 4   Hedgerow Recording Scheme

*See Project No. 71 page 128

Appendix 5   **Frequency Analysis Record**

Locality:											Grid reference:
Date:											
Name of school:											
Description of area:											

Species name	*Quadrat no.*										*Total*
	1	2	3	4	5	6	7	8	9	10	*frequency*
Mayweed	/	—	/	/	—	—	—	—	/	/	5
Shepherds Purse	—	—	/	/	—	/	—	—	/	—	4
Speedwell	/	/	—	—	/	—	/	/	—	/	6
Cleavers	—	—	—	—	/	/	/	—	—	/	4

Project 4

Plymouth Museum Information Inde

by F. R. Gomm   [S–I–A]

An index of information on certain groups of animals in the county of Devon is kept in the Natural History Department of the Plymouth Museum, and help in building up this index would be much appreciated. The index comprises records, photographs, newspaper cuttings, magazine articles, etc., and it is suggested that students, working singly or in groups, take either one animal or a group of animals and collect information as follows (taking for example the mole):

1. Check all past references to the animal in the County and collect them together. This involves working through past numbers of journals such as the *Devonshire Association reports and transactions* (available both at the museum and the library) the *Victoria County History,* natural history books on Devon, Dartmoor, Exmoor, etc., and also any books on moles likely to provide county distributions. References to any fossil material would also be of value here.

2. Make a collection of newspaper cuttings, magazine clippings, photographs, sketches from personal observations, etc.

3. Compile a bibliography of books and articles on moles.

4. Make your own observations.
   Where and when have you seen moles? Molehills? Mole fortresses?
   Were the moles you saw dead or alive?
   If they were dead, why? (road casualty, cat casualty, mole trap?)
   Where have you noticed an absence of moles?
   Parts of Dartmoor? Seashore? City centre?—Why?
   Soil conditions, too acid? Too shallow?
   Too many predators — man, cats, owls, etc.?
   No food?

5. Compile from this information a rough distribution map of the species within the County.

6. Compile a more accurate distribution map of the species within a smaller, defined area—however small.

7. Make patterns of distribution of evidence of activity of the animal, in this case molehills, and accurately plot them with relation to other features such as roads, fences, streams and woods.

8. Suggest reasons for particular distributions recorded, together with any observations on behaviour or life history.

Obviously the headings will vary slightly with individual animals or groups of animals chosen, and help on any chosen topic will be given willingly by the Department.

The following is a list of the headings that so far appear in the index with suggested groupings: work on any would be most valuable.

Headings in Index

Hedgehog

Common shrew
Pygmy shrew
Water shrew

Bat horseshoe
   Noctule
   Leisler's
   Pipistrelle
   Serotine
   Daubenton's

Rabbit
Brown hare

Bank vole
Short-tailed vole
Water vole

House mouse
Long-tailed field mouse
Harvest mouse
Dormouse

Bat (continued)

Whiskered	Black rat
Natterer's	Brown rat
Bechsteins	
Long-eared	Red squirrel
Barbastelle	Grey squirrel
Fox	Atlantic seal
	Common seal
Badger	
	Deer
Otter	
	Porpoises and dolphins
Pine marten	Whales
Stoat	
Weasel	Slow worm
Polecat	Common lizard
	Grass snake
Newts	Adder
Common toad	
Common frog	Fresh water fishes
Marsh frog	

Information to:

Natural History Dept.,
City Museum and Art Gallery,
Plymouth.

Project 5

Ecological Survey

by T. E. Hood   [S–I–A]

Aims

1. To stimulate interest in the local flora and fauna and to cultivate the natural curiosity of the pupils.
2. To instil a scientific attitude of accurate observation and recording.
3. To retain a record of the local flora and fauna and note any changes taking place in the general pattern.
4. To demonstrate to pupils that all the answers are not 'in the book'. There is still room for individual discovery.

Method

1. Three large-scale maps of the area chosen should be made. All three should be lightly colour-washed to indicate the main areas of vegetation, e.g. woodland, pasture, meadow, wasteland, etc. The dominant plants in the areas should be noted.

   Map A
   Using symbols to represent different species, mark off on this map the position of all new species found. The frequency of each species should be recorded in a separate record but can also be shown on the map by using different colours for the symbols.

e.g.	Frequent	. . .	red coloured symbol
	Occasional	. . .	yellow coloured symbol
	Rare	. . .	blue coloured symbol

   Map B
   Using symbols, mark off the positions of bird's nests, ant's nests, mouse burrows, rabbit burrows, etc. A separate record should be kept of any special feeding areas, visiting birds and other animals, giving times of feeding, type of food, etc. Droppings of rabbits and other animals should also be noted. Animal tracks in soft mud and during winter snow will indicate unseen visitations.

   Map C
   This should be treated in the same way as Map B except that it should deal with insects only. The symbol should be placed where the insect was actually seen. A separate record should be kept of the form in which the insect was observed (larva, pupa, or adult) and the food material if feeding.

2. The foregoing information should form the basis for discussion in the classroom. This can be directed in such a way that it emphasizes the close relationships between plants and animals, e.g. food chains, cover, pollination, effects of grazing and faecal deposits.

   Attention can be drawn to illustrations of mimicry, camouflage, bird territory, etc.
   Older pupils should be encouraged to make more detailed studies of small specialized areas such as hedgerows and ponds. Simple transects could be made of suitable subjects.
   The importance of running parallel collections of insects and flowers and the keeping of flower tables cannot be over-emphasized. All collections should be properly labelled with data, name of collector, where found and any other relevant information.
   Should the requisite equipment be available, a local weather record could be kept and simple soil testing experiments carried out.

Suggested books—The Observer Series.

Project 6

A Devon Lane

by F. R. Gomm

[I—A]

The lane habitat — an ideal site for a wide variety of field studies

A Devon lane is a distinct habitat worthy of detailed study and certainly worth conservation effort. It should be possible to classify lanes in a number of different ways, for example:

>
> Historical aspects
> Frequency of usage
> Type of wall (relate to local geology)
> Type of hedge (hazel, thorn, mixed, etc.)
> Height of banks
> Width of road, type of surface, etc.
> Altitude.

The factors affecting animal and plant life in a lane could provide the basis for a very interesting survey project and could possibly be summarized as follows.

Effects of Man

Making up of road (gritting, tarring, etc.)
Actual position of road—does it separate different habitat?
Spraying with insecticides
Hedge-cutting—mechanical or by hand
Hedge clearing—bulldozing or burning
Increased road traffic (casualties?)
Casual water—less puddles and ruts on a made-up road
Picnickers—Fires

>
> Food scraps left around
> Litter
> Parking of cars
> Picking of flowers
> Picking of fruits and nuts.

Effects of Surrounding Countryside

Moorland
Seaside
Farmland or farmyard
Near town, factory or rubbish dump
Near water, salt, fresh, brackish, running, still
Streams or rivers parallel to land or crossing land by ford or bridge.

Other Aspects

Prevailing winds—sheltered or exposed
Steepness—run-off of water
Types of stiles, gates, fences, gateposts
Types of bridge
Stonewalling
Frequency of usage
Census of users—cows, vehicles, pedestrians, etc.

Ecology

This could be treated in a number of ways outlined in any good ecology book. As a suggestion, however, take perhaps a measured length of lane, e.g. 1 km that shows a certain amount of change in character. One starting on the moor, passing through a wood on to farmland might be good to start with. Draw a number of accurate sections at, e.g. five positions to start with, and record the various plants and animals found in the types of habitat contained in the sections, the object being comparison along the length.

The comparison of different types of habitat would lead to the recognition of a number of 'zones', such as the road surface itself, verges on either side, drainage ditches and so on, many of which will occur along the whole length of the road. A study of the fauna and flora of the ditches of the moorland section will provide an interesting comparison with that of the ditch in the shady woodland or farmland. Also the flora and fauna of a hedge will differ from that of a stone wall, and the stone wall in a wood will support different plants from those supported by a stone wall on the moor.

Project 7

Adopting a Study Area

by R. Wilson   [I–A]

An interesting way of integrating ecological techniques, so that they provide a valuable study, is to set up a study area. The advantages are that there is a continuity of study throughout a year: this is not always possible with such features as hedgerows outside a school, because of the external factors which affect the hedgerow. The area, for convenience, should be within the boundary of the school. It should, for preference, contain a tree and a hedge, but any area which can be roped off and left is valuable for this work.

It should, however, be large enough to provide vigorous ecological activity. Since it is assumed that teachers are familiar with ecological techniques, these have been omitted.

1. A number of permanent quadrats should be set up, in various parts of the area (*a*) under tree, (*b*) part shade/part open, (*c*) under hedge, (*d*) in open. Readings should be taken at regular intervals throughout the School year.

2. A line transect should be set up through the area. Readings should be taken at regular intervals.

3. Belt transects should be taken along the length of the line transect, again at regular intervals.

4. Rainfall should be noted (using permanent gauges) (a) under the tree, (b) partly under tree, (c) in the open. Records should be kept, and graphs should be drawn up.

5. An area, within the boundary of the study area, should be mown regularly to show the effect of this.

6. (a) Seeds should be collected from the area. Germination should be tried in the laboratory, seeds should be collected and kept for a number of years to find out successful germination.
(b) Seeds and weights can be estimated for various plants, if seeds are collected from a number of species. Methods of seed dispersal should be noted.
(c) Seeds should be brought in from outside the study area of species which are not normally a feature of the study area.

7. Note the effect of (a) transplantation of species within the study area, (b) transplantation of species from light to shade, (c) transplantation from outside study area of the same species.

8. Light and shade
(a) Measurements should be taken of a number of species growing in various parts of the area: in light and shade, in the open, semi-shade, etc. Are there any species which are (i) confined to shade, (ii) confined to light.
(b) Is there any difference in flowering times of species which are found in light, in shade, in semi-light?

9. Investigate leaf litter: (a) leaf litter from the tree, (b) leaf litter from the hedge.

10. Study movements of animals which are found in the study areas.

11. Worms should be studied, including:
(a) Regeneration.
(b) Worms per square yard (use one per cent solution of formalin sprinkled from watering can, to bring worms to surface). Compare different areas within the study area.
(c) Movement of worms over various surfaces.
(d) Effects of stimuli—light, noise, etc.

12. Photographic records should be kept, including:
(a) Weekly (for preference) photographs of a tree. (Disadvantageous for holidays, although some child can usually be relied on.)
(b) General view of area, taken from same position—either weekly or monthly.
(c) Photographs of specific species to show development.

13. Study the effects of burning on (a) plants; (b) plants in surrounding area; (c) recolonization—do plants come from within study area, or from outside it?

14. Distribution of seeds around tree. There are a number of factors which affect distribution of the seedlings around trees. Strings can be taken from a tree in the four points of the compass, and the number of seedlings along these lines counted. Alternatively an area one foot wide along the lines can be taken.

15. Investigation of animals which are found on (a) the bark and (b) the leaves of the tree—the latter carried out by careful beating.

16. Investigation of the animals found on the flower heads, animals which visit the flowers.

17. The effects of selective weedkillers on plants in the study area, and of the more non-toxic weedkillers (see *Pest Control without Poisons* published by Henry Doubleday Research Association, Bocking, Braintree, Essex).

18. Soil studies:
    (a) make-up of the soil
    (b) water content
    (c) humus content
    (d) sterilization of the soil
     (i) growth of seedlings in this
     (ii) growth of seedlings in soil (treated with something like Jeyes fluid)
    (iii) weedkillers
    (e) bacteria cultures
    (f) soil profiles
    (g) permeability
    (h) pH.

These are a few suggestions, there are many others which can be attempted. In fact almost any biological topic can be brought in, and many of the projects outlined in this book applied to the area adopted.

MAMMALS

Project 8
Animals of your Neighbourhood

by Phyllis Bond   [S]

Aim

To list and map animals seen in your neighbourhood, in preparation for detailed studies of these animals (see Project 9).

Method

Discuss the extent of the area to be studied. This should include all participants' homes and also any nearby places of especial interest, e.g. woods, parks.

Working either individually or in groups, compile a list of animals seen in this area, preferably over a period which includes a weekend.

Draw a large map of the area (not necessarily to scale), marking all woods, hedges, streams, etc. Attach movable labels depicting animals to positions on the map where the animals were seen—'Plastitak' may be better for attachment than drawing pins or cellotape.

Project 9

Detailed Studies on Animals of your Neighbourhood

by Phyllis Bond   [S]

As a result of your work on Project 8 you should have a general picture of the animals which inhabit your neighbourhood, and may already have decided that you want to study a particular animal, or a particular habit, in more detail. The following are a few suggested topics:

Animal homes—Earth, nest, fortress, form, drey, etc.

Wild traits in domestic animals—In addition to observation this could

A badger — although not usually seen during day light, their effect on the country-side they inhabit can be examined

include tracing development of some animals, e.g. the horse from Eohippus to to-day.

Animal feeding habits—Diet, damage to crops, winter stores, etc.

Welcome or Unwelcome?—Survey the uses of animals for work, food, hides, etc., and investigate allegations made against foxes, deer, badgers, rabbits, etc. Methods of control could be looked into.

Effects of the Seasons—Compare conditions of coats, food, habits and behaviour, nests and young, hibernation, etc.

Study of Senses—Note which sense is especially developed—whether equipped with large ears, whiskers, 'radar', strong sense of smell, nocturnal devices, etc. Note reactions to danger and any methods of defence—hedgehog, cats' claws, etc.

Animal terms—Collect and study special words such as brush, slot, herd, reptile, mammal, rodent, carnivora, etc.

A domestic cat may be a readily available subject for detailed study

Project 10

Corrugated Iron/Asbestos Survey

by F. R. Gomm   [S]

If a sheet of corrugated iron or asbestos is left lying on the ground, a number of animals will take up residence beneath it. The types of animals will vary with the time of year—slow worms, lizards and insects in summer, voles in winter, etc. Voles quickly construct beautiful nests and runs, and a plan of these in relation to their caches of food, piles of droppings, etc., would make an interesting study.

Method

Lay a number of sheets of corrugated iron and asbestos in selected areas, e.g. school grounds, waste ground, woodland and open field—but first obtain permission, and be careful not to leave corrugated sheets where they can cause injury to animals; the survey will be more interesting the more the varied the areas. Visit the sheets regularly and record any animals observed and the weather at the time of the visit; replace the sheets carefully. Monthly or fortnightly visits would be sufficient throughout the year. Compare observations with regard to area, time of year and weather.

   Allied to this is a study of animals that live under stones in different areas; these again would change throughout the year. Such a study would be a good theme for nature rambles.

Project 11

Searching for Mammals

by Alfred Leutscher   [S–I]

Aims

To list, and where possible to map, the presence and distribution of mammals within a given area, e.g. in a woodland, a farm area, a village, a riverside, etc.

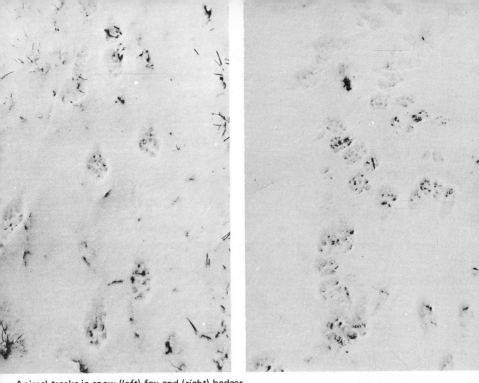

Animal tracks in snow (*left*) fox and (*right*) badger.

Method

Since most mammals are shy, silent and often nocturnal, their presence or passing is often overlooked, so that one needs to look for signs of their passing. These come under four main headings, (*a*) tracks and trails, especially in snow, (*b*) droppings or scats, (*c*) feeding activities, and (*d*)

Animal tracks in damp soil (*left*) heron and (*right*) otter

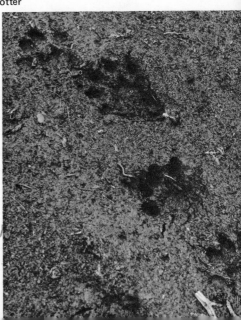

nests or burrows. In addition mammals may be traced by examining pellets of birds-of-prey, and by live-trappings. The last is not recommended unless under careful supervision of a responsible adult.

Recording

This opens up many activities:

(a) Making plaster casts of tracks so as to build up a collection.
(b) The same with food samples, e.g. a nibbled nut or branch, damage to bark, a discarded heap of feathers or bones.
(c) Scats. Droppings each have characteristic shapes, and can be preserved when dried, in small boxes or tubes.
(d) Deserted or used nests (make sure of this) can be kept in boxes.

In time a valuable 'study collection' of the above can be added to the school museum. A personal collection at the Natural History Museum is useful when specimens of all types of 'signs' are brought in for identification.

Benefits

This is an excellent way to get out of doors and act as 'nature detectives', one of the first attributes of a good field-worker.

Your work may also be of help to mammal projects sponsored by adult bodies, e.g. the badger survey and, in Devon, the spread of the mink.

Recommended book: Tracks and signs of British Animals by Alfred Leutscher.

Project 12

The Effects of Man on the Environment

by E. J. White   [S–I]

Man, as the most complex animal, has developed the most complex community and the most complex relations with the environment.

Examples of his effects on the environment are: importation of fertilizer, hoarding phosphorus in gardens and in farm dung heaps, removing rural produce to towns, disposal of waste, modification of climate in towns, and means of rapid transport with the possibility of more rapid spread of plant seeds.

Questions to work on:

For the community around your school list the effects of man on the environment in the form of a diagram. Estimate quantities as far as possible, e.g. the acreage used each year in dumping waste, even if only giving a rough relative rating.

What does man not control in the environment?

What is required to keep the system, i.e. man's use of the environment, going? What would cause it to break down?

If man's environment includes his fellow-man, can you trace any effects of man on living in towns as opposed to rural areas?

Has intensification of agriculture caused some areas to be used less intensively?

Does the system seem logical? How would you improve it?

Project 13

Records of Mole Activity

by H. G. Hurrell   [S—I]

It has been established that every time a mole uses a passage or underground run which has been exposed to light and air by somebody making a hole in the passage, it will stop up the hole with earth. This fact can be used to record when a mole uses a runway.

A few holes should be made with a stick in a chosen run or runs and periodic visits made to ascertain when a mole has passed along the run or runs and thus filled up the holes. Some runs, especially those leading out from a hedge or wood, are likely to be most frequently used.

A useful reference book on this subject is *The Life of the Mole* by Crowcroft.

Project 14

Plotting Mole Hills

by H. G. Hurrell   [S–I]

Another study of mole movement consists of plotting molehills and runs in a field. This should be done in winter, preferably in January, February, and March, as few molehills can be seen in summer.

The only runs which can be seen are those so near the surface that the turf is pushed up to form a ridge as the mole proceeds. Careful records should be made of the time when moles are seen to be actively adding to molehills. This is described as 'heaving'. It would be interesting to see if the time corresponds with the countryman's saying that moles heave at 8 a.m., noon and 4 p.m.

The distribution of the mole in a field or in a whole parish as shown by the presence of molehills would be worth putting on record.

A useful book of reference on this subject is *The Life of the Mole* by Crowcroft.

Caution: Although moles are sometimes a nuisance in the way they 'lift' the soil and push up molehills, they are recognized as being valuable animals due to the number of harmful insects they destroy (see Chapter 5 of the book referred to above).

Project 15

Aggressive and Submissive Behaviour in Horses

by F. A. Turk   [S–I]

Choose for this investigation one of the fields used for grazing the several horses belonging to a riding school. For preference use only a field with at least six individuals, and ask the owner's permission before commencing the investigation. Choose a suitable vantage point from which to feed the horses, e.g. behind the field gate, from behind a wall or, best of all, on an elevation above the field where this is feasible. Ask the owner the names of the horses and learn to recognize them individually. Two or three times a week call the horses over to your chosen station and feed them on such suitable tit-bits as lumps of sugar, apple, carrot or stale bread. Note their behaviour.

1. Does one drive the others away (dominant)?
2. Which of the others feeds most in the absence of the dominant one?
3. Is the same horse dominant for all group situations in the field?
4. Is the dominant one the biggest?
5. Does the dominant one change over a period of weeks?
6. Is there any observable difference in the gait (manner of walking, etc.) or stance (way tail is held, etc.) in the dominant animals?
7. What happens to a new horse when it is first introduced into the field?
8. If possible compare your results with similar situations in pigs, sheep or poultry.
9. Make notes of your observations every time you feed the horses and eventually write a short account of the group.

Project 16

The Distribution of Mammals

by G. B. Corbet   [I–A]

The Mammal Society is currently conducting an enquiry with the very limited object of preparing distribution maps of mammals in the British Isles on the basis of the 10 km squares of the National Grid. However, it is also an object of the enquiry to encourage more local recording in greater detail, e.g. on the basis of 1 km squares.

The simplest way of compiling maps is to use a sheet of squared paper for each species, letting the smallest squares represent the 1 km squares. Topographical features can be drawn on a single transparent overlay or on each map. Each filled-in square on the map should be backed up by a card or record sheet giving the evidence on which the record is based and the data. Records may be based upon sighting of an animal; the finding of a dead animal or of a skull; or on indirect evidence like droppings, tracks or burrows, provided the species can be conclusively deduced.

Record sheets and explanatory leaflets are available from Dr. G. B. Corbet, British Museum (Natural History), London S.W.7. It is requested that all correspondence with the Society be conducted by the teacher or by *one* representative of the school who will be responsible for vetting and passing on to the Society the limited selection of records that are relevant to the national enquiry.

References

CORBET, G. B., *The Identification of British Mammals* (London: British Museum (Natural History), 1964).
SOUTHERN, H. N. (ed.) *The Handbook of British Mammals* (London: Blackwell, 1964).

Project 17

Identification of Small Mammals Trapped in Bottles

by W. O. Copland   [I–A]

Vast numbers of bottles, chiefly milk bottles, are left empty in the countryside. A look around any camp site, lay-by, viewpoint or other place frequented by the public on holiday will usually reveal hidden treasures. Inside bottles which have lain around for any length of time will be found a muddy broth, evil smelling and rich in accumulated insects, woodlice and snails.

Handle the bottles with gloved hands; they can be collected up in boxes for later examination but be sure to record the precise localities with Grid Reference Numbers. Among the invertebrate remains will be found often skulls, jaws, and other skeletal fragments belonging to unfortunate mice, voles or shrews which have entered them and been

Two of the small mammals which may be trapped during this project (*left*) bank vole and (*right*) pygmy shrew

unable to escape due to the slippery glass and the tilt of the bottle. One quart milk bottle in Essex contained a total of twenty-eight small mammals!

Pour the contents of each bottle through a sieve into a plastic bowl and carefully examine the remains, picking out skulls and jaws for identification under hand lens or low-power binocular microscope. It is important that the grinding surfaces of the teeth should be clean as these are often the key to identification. A jaw can be mounted on a small piece of plasticine for observation. Using the keys in Project 18 and/or the illustrations that follow, species can be identified although it is not possible to distinguish Woodmice (*Apodemus sylvaticus*) from Yellow-necked mice (*Apodemus flavicollis*). However, experts at the British Museum (Natural History) are trying to separate these two species and *Apodemus* skulls could be sent there. Among the species known to be trapped in this way are Common, Pigmy and Water Shrews; Bank and Short-tailed Voles; Wood, Yellow-necked, House and Harvest Mice. The distribution of our native British Mammals, especially the smaller and less demonstrative species, is still imperfectly known and your records will be welcomed by

The Mammal Society Distribution Scheme,
c/o Mammal Section, British Museum (Natural History),
Cromwell Road, London, S.W.7.

who are preparing maps for all native species.

Remains can be mounted on cards and made into an exhibit to show how dangerous it is to leave bottles lying in the countryside. You could also compare the frequency of different species collected from bottles in your locality with those found in owl pellets. A competition to see who can find the bottle with the most trapped animals in it is always a possibility! Examination of the invertebrate remains and compilation of a key to them could be attempted. Some surprises such as one *Pisidium* and eleven *Planorbis* snails extracted from a bottle near a pool in Dorset, can be expected.

References

CORBET, G. B., *The Identification of British Mammals* (London, British Museum (Natural History), 1964), pp. 27–40.
SOUTHERN, H. N. (ed.), *Handbook of British Mammals* (London, Blackwell, 1964), p. 114.
MORRIS, P., 'Glass Coffins', *Animals*, 1965, **7**, 454–455.
MORRIS, P. and HARDER, J. F., 'The occurrence of small mammals in discarded bottles', *Proc. Zool. Soc.*, Lond., 1965, **145**, 148–153.

Project 18

Identification of Small Mammal Skulls

[I–A]

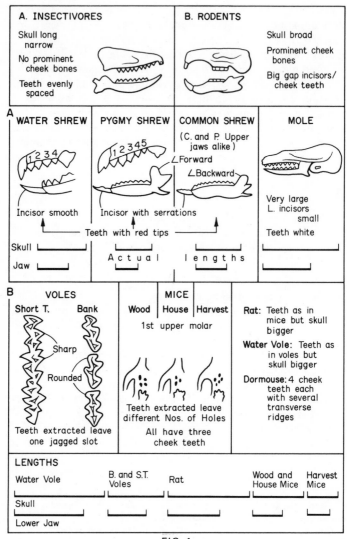

A. INSECTIVORES

Skull long narrow

No prominent cheek bones

Teeth evenly spaced

B. RODENTS

Skull broad

Prominent cheek bones

Big gap incisors/ cheek teeth

A

WATER SHREW

Incisor smooth

PYGMY SHREW

Incisor with serrations

Teeth with red tips

COMMON SHREW

(C. and P. Upper jaws alike)

∠Forward

∠Backward

MOLE

Very large L. incisors small

Teeth white

Skull

Jaw

Actual lengths

B

VOLES

Short T.   Bank

Sharp

Rounded

Teeth extracted leave one jagged slot

MICE

Wood | House | Harvest

1st upper molar

Teeth extracted leave different Nos. of Holes

All have three cheek teeth

Rat: Teeth as in mice but skull bigger

Water Vole: Teeth as in voles but skull bigger

Dormouse: 4 cheek teeth each with several transverse ridges

LENGTHS

Water Vole   B. and S.T. Voles   Rat   Wood and House Mice   Harvest Mice

Skull

Lower Jaw

FIG. 1

N.B. Amphibian skulls have no teeth and are very flat. Reptilian skulls have minute teeth, and fall apart easily, therefore are rarely found whole.

Project 19

Deer

by F. J. Taylor Page   **[I–A]**

Every county in England and Scotland has deer within its boundaries.
There are six species, one or more of which may be found wild or in
parks: Red, Fallow, Japanese Sika, Roe, Chinese Water Deer and
Reeves's Muntjac. I have given them in order of their size. They can be
identified with the help of *The Field Guide to British Deer* published by
the Mammal Society and obtainable from the Publications Secretary,
British Deer Society, Grey Plovers, Hendon Wood Lane, Mill Hill,
N.W.7. You should ask your local library to get a copy for you.

Deer can be studied fairly easily in parks, where their behaviour is
little different from that in the wild. Permission can usually be obtained
from the estate agent if you wish to make regular visits for scientific
observation. Make friends with the keeper and get him to help you. But
stalking and watching really wild deer is much more exciting and
rewarding. You will find out how to do this in the Field Guide. Nowa-
days many of the forests managed by the Forestry Commission have
deer observation towers established at strategic positions in the rides,
and it is possible to obtain permission to use these for deer study. A
school might ask for permission to build its own hide, or transportable
high seat. Designs for these can also be found in the Field Guide.

The first and most obvious thing to do, however, is to find out what
species of deer exist near to your home. A study of the tracks in the
forest rides will usually give satisfactory evidence. Regular visits and
watching from a hide will eventually provide the information that you want.
Be sure to follow the advice given in the Field Guide, taking particular
care to avoid noise of any kind or allowing the wind to take your scent
in the direction in which you are stalking.

Try to find out as much as you possibly can about the species of deer
you have discovered. You will find that there is still a very great deal
that is unknown. Here are some of the lines of investigation you might
follow up:

(i) Find out exactly how a deer spends its day. How much time is
     spent on feeding, sleeping or just resting?

(ii) By observation record the different food plants used. Does the
     use of particular plants vary from season to season? What is the
     favourite food plant? Does the occurrance of particular plants
     seem to determine where the deer are found?

(iii) What changes in behaviour occur from season to season?

(iv) Record the ratio of bucks to does in a herd of park deer. How does this vary from year to year?
      What steps are taken to keep the total population within reasonable limits? Why?

 (v) Make a tape recording of the sounds made by one deer species. Then try to use the recording to attract deer to you.

(vi) Deer are said to like music. Use a portable radio or tape recorder and discover what kinds of music appear to attract and what kinds fail in this respect.

(vii) Discover how long it takes a deer to change its coat from winter to summer condition and vice versa.

(viii) What large scale and small scale movements do the deer make? Fallow deer, for example, can be found in one area during part of the year, and then suddenly they disappear. Where do they go and what attracts them to a new area?

(ix) What happens to cast antlers? Search for them at the right time of the year, for each species. Get a forester to give you an old cast antler. Put it out in a deer forest and see what happens to it week by week.

 (x) Make a study of the amount of damage done in a young plantation by roe or fallow deer. This involves careful watching, tree counting and much perseverance. How and when is the damage done? What are the peak times of activity, and why is the damage caused?

If you want further advice and help, write to
F. J. Taylor Page, British Deer Society,
Low Hay Bridge, Bouth-by-Ulverston, Lancs.

Project 20

Mammalian Droppings

by Roger Burrows   [I–A]

Whilst not being an aesthetically pleasing study, an investigation of mammalian faeces can be most rewarding in discovering not only the diet of the particular species but also its behavioural characteristics such as territorial marking.

Much of the following can be adapted to the study of many species; the fox is the one suggested for study here.

The first requirements are to collect the fox droppings at regular intervals preferably once per week from a selected area that is accessible and over which there is free access (or permission to use the area is obtained). The area should be thoroughly covered on each visit and it is essential to have a large scale map on at least 10 cm to the kilometre scale. Do not choose too big an area, experience shows that an area of about two square kilometres is more than adequate. As far as the fox is concerned it does not matter what sort of country or urban area is chosen as the fox has very catholic habitat requirements.

Having chosen the area all hedges round the fields should be walked and a careful look kept for fox footprints in loose earth (especially in

Fox feeding on chicken bait

the dead furrows at the field edge) and also, of course, for droppings. The position of each scat (a convenient term for the dropping) should be plotted on the map and the scat placed in a small polythene bag for later examination. Gaps in hedges are particularly productive of scats in mid-winter, and so are slight rises above the general ground surface such as a large stone, a patch of burnt vegetation, the carcass of a dead animal or even a block of salt put out for cattle. A note should be kept in a field book of the exact position of each scat collected.

At the end of each month it will be found instructive to prepare a simple traced outline of the study area with the droppings plotted onto it. In this way the change, if any, in position and number of the monthly collection of scats will become evident.

A well-established movement pattern of the local foxes will soon become apparent and watches for foxes can then be attempted using a convenient tree or other concealment near the runways.

Analysis of the droppings calls for very simple equipment and technique. The droppings are placed in a large kitchen sieve and washed well with running water, and any sediment that comes through the sieve is collected in an enamel dish to be examined for earthworm *chaetae*. The washed remains in the sieve are then turned out into a clean white enamel dish and sorted with mounted needles and forceps. Most items in the scat will be easily recognized macroscopically with a little experience but the hair and feather remains will require microscope identification and use of a key (Day, 1966). If the key cannot be readily obtained, one can be produced by looking at hairs from known small mammals, mounted on slides as a reference collection, and discovering diagnostic features of the species. It is a great aid to identification if a cross section of the prey hair is made. This can be done very simply by means of a cork, needle and cotton plus a safety razor blade.

A threaded needle is passed through a small piece of cork and then returned through the original hole, leaving a loop of cotton protruding from the surface of the cork. A small bunch of hair is then placed in the loop and pulled into the body of the cork by pulling the cotton on the needle side of the cork. A small amount of the hair should be left just above the level of the cork. A razor blade is now used to cut thin sections in the usual way. The sections are mounted dry on a microscope slide and examined. Typical cross sections are readily observed by this technique and prey species identified.

The percentage occurrence of each item in the diet can be calculated on the basis of the number of scats containing the item as a percentage number of scats collected for that month, or week or year. A monthly determination will be most informative in giving an indication of a change in diet with the seasons and availability of food. This latter point is very important, and during the weekly visits to the area a careful note should be kept of what potential fox food is available and where. To determine the availability of small mammal prey, live trapping should be carried out periodically.

1. Is there any marked monthly variation in the number and distribution of the scats?

2. Is there any evidence to suggest that the scats are being used to mark territory at any time of the year?

3. What parts of the habitat are used most frequently for defaecation?

4. Is there a correlation between availability of fox food in the area and its occurrence in the scats?

5. Try to establish the amount of damage that the foxes in your area do to livestock, and how much of the remains of domestic animals found in the scats could have come from carrion. Check any local reports of fox damage and see how the reported losses fit in with your own findings.

6. Collect scats from earths with cubs and see if there is any difference between the diet of adults and cubs.

7. Foxes readily come to bait and it is worth thinking about possible means of marking the bait so that it can be recognized when it appears later in the scats.

8. Check the food remains found outside earths in your area; does this study give an unbalanced idea as to the total diet of the fox as obtained from your study of scats in the same area?

9. Try to work out the fluctuations in the local population of foxes over the seasons and the years by your study of scats and other field signs.

10. What is the role of the fox in the countryside, if any?

11. Try to get your results published in your local Natural History Society Journal or some other Journal.

We still know very little about the normal day-to-day lives of British mammals in the wild. This is mainly due to the difficulties of observation, but using the technique mentioned above much useful information can be obtained as well as training the eye, nose and mind.

Further advice or information can be obtained from Roger Burrows, 'Breanco', Goonvrea, St. Agnes, Cornwall.

References

BURROWS, R. S., *Wild Fox* (Newton Abbott, David and Charles, 1968).

DAY, M. G., 'Identification of hairs and feather remains in the gut and faeces of stoats and weasels', *Journal of Zoology*, 1966, **148**, 201—217.

LEUTSCHER, A., *Tracks and Signs of British Animals* (London, Macmillan, 1960).

LOCKIE, J. D., 'Estimation of the food of foxes', *Wildlife Management, 1959,* **23**, 224—227.

SOUTHERN, H. N. (ed.), *Handbook of British Mammals* (London, British Museum (Natural History), 1964).

Project 21

A Study of the Diet of Bats

by John Hooper   [A]

Little is known, in any detail, of the diet of individual species of bat, and indeed, such diet may well vary from one district to another. Any knowledge that could be gained on this subject would be useful.

It is visualized that work to gain such knowledge would involve:

(a) The search for and location of one, or perhaps two haunts used by bats (e.g. house roofs, barns, churches, maybe in one of the school buildings.)

(b) The identification of the species concerned. (Expert help may be needed here.)

(c) Observation to establish hunting and feeding habits. This would probably require a lot of patience and might well be discouraging. Some bats feed on the wing, others take food back to the shelter of a haunt (though the latter may only be temporary). If such a bat 'dining room' can be found, beneath it there will also be found discarded, uneaten portions of their insect food.

Long-eared bat

(*d*) Collection of these uneaten bits of insect for identification. In some cases it may be necessary to obtain expert (e.g. museum) assistance.

(*e*) Preparation of an exhibit to illustrate the results—photographs, drawings, maps, actual specimens of the insect concerned.

Note: This is a summer project, and a difficult one. It may indeed prove too difficult, but it is at least worth trying. Great care would need to be taken to observe the bats without disturbing them. Excessive disturbance might cause the bats to move to another haunt, or change their habits—in which case the project would come to an abrupt halt.

Results from investigations into this project should be sent to: Mr. John Hooper, 34 Richmond Road, Staines, Middlesex, who should be contacted if expert help is required.

Project 22

A Study of the Hunting/Flying Habits of Bats

by John Hooper   [A]

Bats leave their daytime haunts at dusk to go hunting, and possibly also in the early morning. Some species seem to stay on the wing for many hours, others for only about half an hour. Little detailed observation has been made to make precise records of such movements, and to see whether the behaviour of each species is consistent, or if such behaviour varies with the time of year. The work would involve:

(*a*) Location of one or more haunts used by bats.

(*b*) Positive identification of the species in each such haunt. (Warning—several species may inhabit the same house roof.)

(*c*) A watching system (possibly some rota arrangement could be made, to cover as many evenings as possible and spread out over the spring and summer months and as late as possible into the autumn), with the object of recording:

    (i) The earliest date when the bats cease hibernating and start to hunt.

    (ii) The latest date in autumn, or winter, on which the bats are seen hunting.

    (iii) The time of emergence from the roost, and time of return.

(iv) Relevant data, such as time of sunset, weather conditions, e.g. rain or strong winds, etc.

(d) For bats which emerged while there was some daylight left, it might be possible to make some measurements of prevailing light intensity, e.g. using a cadmium cell meter.

(e) For schools well equipped scientifically, the possibility is suggested of designing and constructing some photo-cell counting/timing device to record the emergence of bats from a haunt, if the latter is suitably placed. It would probably be necessary to use an infra-red beam, as a visible light beam would discourage the bats from normal emergence.

(f) A plot of emergence and return time against date, or time for sunset, over a long period, even if only for one species, to see if any pattern emerged, would be extremely interesting.

Note: This again is not an easy project, and might well be combined with the previous project.

It would involve a tremendous amount of observation, and to be worthwhile, it would need to be persistent observation, night after night, regardless of weather, so that a *full* story of the bats' hunting habits can be built up.

As with Project 21 it would be necessary to observe the bats without disturbing them; otherwise the bats might be caused to move to another haunt, thus causing the earlier observations to be wasted.

Results from investigations into this project should be sent to Mr. John Hooper, 34 Richmond Road, Staines, Middlesex, who also should be contacted if expert help is required.

Special Warning: It cannot be emphasized too strongly with both the foregoing projects: the first and most important consideration must be the welfare of the bats being studied.

As has been said above, excessive disturbance will inevitably lead to desertion of the haunt by the bats, and if this happens the student concerned will have failed in the first duty to the species under investigation.

BIRDS

Project 23

Study of a Bird

by K. W. Dendle   [S]

Quietness is essential when birdwatching, and sudden movements must not be made. **Do not damage any nests or take eggs, or make a 'road' into a nesting site** during your study.

Select the bird you wish to study and try to answer the following questions about it:

General

What name or names has the bird you are studying?
Find out the names of other birds of the same 'family'.
How big is it? (large, small or medium).
What colour is its plumage? Draw and colour a picture of it.
What are the differences in colouring of the male and female?

Head, Legs and Feet

What is the shape of the bird's beak?
Is it large or small? Make a drawing.
Are its legs long or short, thick or thin?
What colour are they?
How many toes has the bird? How are they arranged? Make a drawing.

Movement

How does the bird move on the ground? (quickly, bobbing, etc.).
How does it move in the air? (straight, undulating, soaring).
How does it alight and how does it take off?
How does it rest, and where?

Feeding

What have you seen it feeding on?
How does it feed?
If you have seen it drinking, describe how it does so.
Introduce various food stuffs to its locality and see which the bird eats.

A tit feeding on one of its sources of fat — the rich cream which collects at the top of the milk

Nesting

In this part of your work, take care not to frighten the mother bird.
Make only brief visits. Watch from a little distance away.
Where was the nest? (hedge, bush, tree, ground, etc.)
What shape, and what was it made of?
How many eggs were laid?
What was their shape, size and colour?
When did they hatch?
Approximately how long was incubation?
What were the nestlings fed on?
How often did the parents bring food? Time them.
Did the male help with feeding?
When did the young leave the nest?

Habits

Is it a migratory bird?
Does it gather in flocks?
Is it pugnacious, timid, shy or friendly?

Song

Does it sing? If so, where and when?
Does it repeat the same notes or does it sing different ones?
Does anything or another kind of bird agitate the song?
Try to write down what it seems to say.

Project 24

The Flight of Birds

by D. Theak   [S]

Aim

To study birds in flight in such a way as to encourage the children's
powers of observation and to stimulate in the children an appreciation
of the beauty of the flight of birds, helping them to see how the
structure of each type of bird fits it for its own particular kind of life.

General Notes on Method

The project should run for the whole year for top class juniors. At least
six lesson periods each term should be given up to this topic which
should be interspersed with other forms of Nature Study. The project
should be carried out partly out-of-doors at suitable places for watching
birds, and partly indoors. For out-door work each child should have a
'Flight Notebook' for jotting down observations. For their permanent
records they should have exercise books with drawing pages and lined
pages alternately.

Part of the Nature Table in the classroom should be reserved for an
exhibition of types of feathers. As the children's interest grows, this
exhibition will need to be extended, with pictures of birds in flight,
which the children will find in magazines, newspapers and B.B.C.
pamphlets, to be mounted and displayed on the wall.

Before the project is introduced, the teacher should be collecting
any undamaged wings, tail feathers and body feathers of birds found
to have died of cold or to have had fatal accidents. The children can
also begin collecting feathers beforehand, not only of wild birds, but
also from poultry.

Charts of birds, such as those obtainable from the Royal Society for
the Protection of Birds, The Lodge, Sandy, Bedfordshire, are invaluable for identification and should be kept on the classroom wall while
the project is in progress.

Introducing the Topic

Ask children what they have noticed about different types of birds'
flight and lead up to discussion on such points as the gliding flight of
gulls, the soaring of the buzzard, direct steady flight of the crow tribe,
undulating flight of many small birds, such as finches and tits.

How do birds such as swans and ducks alight on water?
How do they take off?

How does a bird of prey hold its wings when it dives rapidly through the air?

Stimulate interest and encourage the children to observe and report on this type of thing.

Suggestions to the Teacher for Planning Outdoor Work

After a short preliminary talk has been given, telling the children what particularly to look out for, outings should be made, according to the locality of the school, to such places as:

(a) A sea front, where gulls can be seen wheeling round while being fed. Observe the birds' mastery of the air, the way they steer, using their balance by adjustment of the wings, and the way they 'brake' by presenting a larger surface of body, wings and tail to the air ahead.

(b) A reservoir, lake or pond, where swans, ducks and more gulls can be watched taking flight and alighting, and where feathers can be picked up at preening places.

(c) An estuary, especially between the months of September and March, when wading birds and various ducks are numerous.

(d) Cliffs, where gulls and jackdaws are coming and going, and playing in the rising air-currents.

(e) Fields, where gulls follow the tractor, when ploughing is in progress; where winter flocks of birds, such as lapwings, are feeding and flying with great manoeuvrability, or where snipe can be seen rising with their zig-zag flight, also where the tumbling flight of lapwings in their spring and summer nesting places can be studied.

Suggestions for Indoor Work

When the children have had one or two outings, have begun to be aware of some of the wonderful aspects of birds' flight, and have made some notes about the varieties of flight, they will be ready to do written work in their Nature Notebooks, illustrating this with drawings.

Note: Most children find it extremely difficult to do original drawings of living birds, especially in flight, but are keen to illustrate their written work by copying coloured pictures or photographs from bird books or charts.

They enjoy drawing and painting feathers of various birds, with pastels on coloured paper, or with water-colours on white background. Feathers can also be mounted with cellotape on sheets of coloured paper and labelled, for the classroom exhibition.

The making of anthologies of poems about birds in flight can be a part of the project. There are a great many poems to be found, referring to the joy of the skylark's song and flight, the power of the buzzard's soaring flight, the grace of the swallow, the wonder of migratory flights and so on.

Introduction on Simple Scientific Study

While the work is developing, the teacher can introduce some scientific work in an indoor lesson from time to time, on these subjects:

1. Structure of a bird's wing

It should be shown how the arm, wrist and hand are adapted. Diagrams can be drawn on the blackboard, showing how the primary and secondary feathers are attached to the bones. Power to work the wings is provided by strong muscles running from the humerus to the breast bone. The downward stroke of the wing is the most important. The resistance of the air is turned into support. A diagram of a bat's wing should be shown, for comparison. Real wings of birds should be studied closely and the wonderful over-lapping of the feathers noted.

2. Structure of feathers

(a) Flight feathers of wing and tail should be studied with actual specimens, noting that each has a solid central shaft rising from a light, hollow quill and are firm and strong, with web or vane formed by numerous slender barbs, linked together by minute interlocking barbules. (A sketch of these, much enlarged, should be shown on the board and children can detect their presence on their own flight feathers best, by parting the web, then smoothing it together, noting how the barbules instantly fall into position again, so that the web forms a surface through which air cannot pass.)

(b) Down feathers, for warmth, no central shaft or interlocking barbules.

3. How each type of bird is built for the kind of life it lives

Suggestions for this lesson and points for the children to look out for:

(a) Generally, birds with prolonged and strong flight and those seeking their living in the air have longer and narrower wings than those who make short flights. Migrants show this difference when compared with those that are non-migratory.

(b) Birds living in woods and in other cover usually have shorter, often more rounded wings and weaker flight, not having to fly far for food, or for escaping from enemies, i.e. woodpeckers, jay, tree creeper.

(c) Birds having to make quick dives and turns in the air, either for catching prey, including insect food, or for escaping from enemies, generally have longer pointed wings and sometimes pointed, forked tails, i.e. swallow, house-martin, sand-martin, swift, terns or 'sea-swallows', spotted fly-catcher. Snipe and other waders have pointed wings for quick escape from enemies in the open.

(d) The wings of birds of prey follow these general rules, the kestrel, hunting in the open, having long tail and long wings, delicately pointed for steering and keeping balance while hunting against wind; the sparrow-hawk, dodging around trees and bushes, not being impeded by length of wings, flying quickly on short wings, using tail for steering and checking flight.

(e) Compare the noticeable 'keel' of the heron with the complete lack of this development of the breast-bone in the ostrich which no longer possesses the power of flight. The heron has strong muscles with particularly large expanse of wing, for carrying large supplies of food in his gullet for long distances, to feed the young. (The teacher will probably find it worthwhile to have more than one lesson on this subject of adaptation for special purposes.)

Miscellaneous Points

These might be introduced when opportunities occur.

The movements of the wing are rather like the action of oars in rowing. If a large bird, such as a heron, is watched while flying slowly, it will be seen to form a figure-of-eight in the air with each wing, the lower loop being smaller than the upper. Other birds do this but the movement cannot be detected in smaller birds; the smaller the wing, the more strokes are needed per minute. Movement is upwards, forwards and downwards, then slightly backwards. Upward movement is so marked in pigeons that they clap their wings together over their backs when taking flight. (This may be to warn the flock of danger as they have no alarm note.) Partridges also make a great clatter with their wings when rising, but owls have absolutely silent flight, for hunting, this being made possible by thread-like developments of the barbules on the wing feathers, muffling sound. Children enjoy looking out for the spreading of the bastard wings, or thumb wings, of birds when alighting. These are not noticeable in small birds, but can be seen well when pigeons alight in parks, or gulls on embankments, rooks and jack-daws on nearby objects. These small extra wings are raised momentarily to present more surface to the air to check flight.

Project 25

Birds and Berries

by W. Brett Hornby   [S]

It is commonly observed that birds choose the order in which they use
the hedgerow 'berries' for food. An interesting record could be made
of the dates and weather conditions relating to the use of various types
of 'berry'. Results might show whether some fruits are resorted to only
in the absence of others or whether they appear to become palatable
after a period of ripening.

In every case it would be useful to know whether the bird species
themselves are always the same for one type of plant at a particular
time.

This is a prolonged investigation, taking several years to make comparisons, but each year would in itself provide a reason for looking at
and noticing the birds' behaviour.

Project 26

Operation Starling

by K. W. Dendle   [S—I]

This is an account of a survey undertaken by a group of top juniors in
a rural primary school.

It has been noted by the children that large flocks of starlings passed
over the school at approximately the same time each day, so it was
decided to plot the flight paths and to find out where the birds went.
Several problems had to be overcome at the outset, and thanks are due
to Mr. Jenkyn, H.M.I., for his initial plan of campaign; to Mr. Hurrell and
Mr. Watkins for their advice concerning the estimation of flock sizes;
and to headmasters and children of the contributory schools who
helped in the scheme.

After consultation it was decided that other schools would have to
be approached in order to help to follow flocks across country, and
with this in mind the children wrote to neighbouring schools seeking
their cooperation. Four schools showed an interest, but unfortunately
only two of these were anywhere along the estimated flight routes. The

other two were too far north, and in positions against the sea; however, their recordings proved of value in the final assessment.

Worksheets were prepared with the following headings:

State of weather; direction of wind; direction flock sighted; time sighted; time of disappearance from view; direction of disappearance; estimated size of flock; peculiarities in shape of flock.

The recorders were asked to be on duty on given dates twice weekly between the hours of 3.30 and 4.00 p.m. Observations began on November 24 and finished on December 15, 1966.

The question of estimating the number of birds caused some thought, and after making enquiries it was decided to adopt the method given by Mr. Hurrell—count the leading 20 birds, gain an impression of their mass and count on in twenties to 100. Thereafter 100 was used as the unit. This method was found workable, and it is hoped reasonable accuracy was obtained.

Observations were made by posting two 'look-outs' who reported the flocks, while a third member called out the time, another estimated size, and a fifth did the recording. All work was carried out from the same place on each occasion.

During the time work was progressing it was read in the local press that the foresters at the neighbouring forest were waging a war against the starlings at the site of the roost. Fearing that the birds would be moved by the attack, the children found out the position of the roost and visited it. This was before contributory schools had forwarded their papers.

The visit to the roost took place on December 16 and the children were in position by 3.30 p.m. The first flocks came from the east at 3.57 but they flew on overhead to disappear flying westward. The first birds to settle at the roost were timed at 4.15 p.m. Thereafter the sky was literally black with birds. The main arc of approach covered the zone from N.N.E. to S.S.E. Several thousand birds did however come in from the west and south west, and it was thought these were early arrivals who had gone beyond the roost, possibly for more feeding as it was not quite dusk. This theory was later supported by a coach driver who reported having seen a large number of starlings gathering in a field almost due west of the roost. The noise made by the birds was likened by one child to the noise of a rushing river. Through glasses the children watched the birds settling in for the night. There appeared to be quite a period of internal movement from branch to branch, and from tree to tree. The roost was situated in a six acre plantation of spruce, and foresters said that the whole section had been ruined.

When finally the reports came in the children were able to draw on a map the general direction of the routes taken by the flocks passing near to the four schools, and the lines converged onto Map Reference SS 275186—the site of the roost visited.

What else did they find out? The only two flocks that could possibly have been plotted by two different schools were both on the same day.

The assumptions were based on the following data:

	Monkleigh	Parkham
Estimated size of flock	2/3000	3000
Time spotted	(Going) 3·45 p.m.	(Coming) 3·57 p.m.

The difference in time was 12 minutes. The distance (direct line) between Monkleigh and Parkham is 4½ miles. They calculated the speed of flight by timing flocks over a measured distance of 70 yards in a field opposite the school and found the average to be 28 m.p.h. This would allow distance MP to be covered in approximately 10 minutes. Parkham lies west of Monkleigh and slightly north of that school's flight route to the roost, but on the day in question there was a strong south westerly wind blowing and we think that this could have accounted for th drift northwards. The other flock was estimated by both schools as being 1500 strong, and the difference in times was the same as for the larger flock.

The schools are all perched high on the N.W. plateau where winds are frequently of gale force. On the days when winds were of force 5 or more, the flocks were exceedingly small—in fact none over the 200 mark. When these small flocks went over they were seen to be hedge-hopping. On three occasions flocks were noticed using valleys to make their way westwards.

The children still notice the starlings going home to roost, but as one said quite recently, 'They are later now aren't they?' It would appear that the foresters have lost their battle for the present as the flight routes are still along the familiar E.S.E. to W.S.W. lanes.

Project 27

Nesting Preferences of Common Birds

by F. A. Turk   [S–I]

It would seem that not all trees are used equally commonly by any species of bird; moreover, the kind of tree preferred may differ over the whole range of some species. Recording the trees in which the commoner types have built their nests may reveal some interesting patterns of choice. A useful species with which to commence is the rock, a bird whose chief preference seems to vary in different counties.

Method

1. Record all occurrences of the nests of the one or more species which have been chosen for study. Suggested species: rook, magpie, woodpigeon or wren. Tabulate these, commencing with the commonest choice of tree, and working down the list.

2. Endeavour to determine the number of young raised in each nest in each type of tree.

3. Calculate the height of each nest above the ground.

4. Calculate and record the height of the tree and its condition.

Questions

1. Can you make any general statements from the results?

2. What factors do you think might govern the results?

3. What methods would you adopt to check your results?

Under the Wild Bird Protection Act 1967 it is an offence to disturb nests (or birds near them) of certain species and of all species in certain areas. Teachers contemplating any project on birds should obtain copies of this act and the 1954 Act to which it refers.

Project 28

Bird Song

by H. G. Hurrell   [S—I—A]

This project has the advantage that it can be carried out in almost any environment; gardens and parks may be better places than woods and hedgerows because birds in the former are used to people. Spring is the best time of year to study bird songs.

Method

First discuss bird songs in the classroom, if possible with the use of recordings. Prepare cards with the names and/or drawings of, say, half a dozen birds which are resident in your area. Select a place where several birds are singing and wait there quietly. When you identify a bird which is singing clearly, tick the species on your card. After you have become familiar with the songs of resident birds, you can try to recognize the songs of migrants. Birds also have alarm notes and other calls; these may be more difficult to identify than song.

If you have the use of a tape recorder, you may, under suitable conditions, be able to record bird songs and calls, and perhaps the dawn chorus, for yourselves.

Project 29

Communal Roosts for Birds

by H. G. Hurrell   [S–I–A]

During the winter months flocks of starlings, rooks, jackdaws and gulls can be seen during the late afternoon flying across the country to their nightly roosting places.

Sometimes these roosts can be found by clever detective work. Plot the spot where the flying birds are first seen with the help of an Ordnance Survey map, noting the direction, time and weather conditions. Study the map ahead of the line of flight and pick out a road not too far away over which you think they may fly.

Try to get there the next day at the same time to see if they do fly over the spot you have picked and, if so, again record the direction of flight, time and weather conditions. Copy the relevant part of the map and plot the flight lines with arrows. Repeat the exercise as long as is necessary to find the roost. If you miss them one evening you will have to try again nearer the previous day's sighting spot to try to pick up their flight line.

It will not matter if you have to miss some days in between each observation, even once a week may eventually lead you to the roost.

When the roost is found see if you can find methods of estimating the number of birds using it. Information about the catchment area from which a roost draws its birds is useful. Records of major roosts each year in Devon would be gratefully received by:

H. G. Hurrell, Moorgate, S. Brent, Devon.

Project 30

Birds of Prey Census

by H. G. Hurrell   [S–I–A]

Mr. Ian Prestt of the Nature Conservancy, Monkswood Experimental
Station is continuing part of his 1964 Bird-of-Prey Programme into
1965.

This consists of a census of three birds of prey—the Kestrel, the
Buzzard and the Sparrowhawk—and can be carried out by lone workers
or groups of observers. All that is necessary is for the observer to decide
on a given research area and visit it regularly—say one weekly visit of
three hours—and record the number of sightings of each species of bird-
of-prey in question.

It is sometimes difficult to distinguish between consecutive sightings
of the same bird and different birds appearing about the same time.
This is not important, however, providing a system is agreed and kept to
by all observers. Most people endeavour to record different birds as
distinct from several records of the same bird.

Large-scale flight silhouettes could be made by teacher and class to
familiarize pupils with the three species. These could be copied from
Collins Field Guide to the Birds of Britain and Europe.

Records should be sent to Ian Prestt, Monks Wood Experimental
Station, Abbots Ripon, Huntingdon.

Project 31

Tests for Tits on Bird Tables

by H. G. Hurrell   [S–I–A]

There are many interesting ways of testing the ability of birds which
visit the bird table. Perhaps the simplest test is provided by suspending
a peanut (unsalted) by means of a thread from a horizontal perch. (A
needle passed through the nut with a knot at the end of the thread is a
satisfactory way of attaching the nut.)

At first the thread may have to be short, otherwise tits are likely to
try direct action by clinging to the nut. It will also help to initiate the
birds if at first they can easily reach the nut from the perch. When the
thread is lengthened the tits should raise the nut by alternately hoisting

the thread with its bill and holding it firm under a foot. It has been debated as to whether this is a case of intelligent anticipation or merely a more or less automatic succession of events.

One of the most revealing tests is the 'Perspex Test' (Figure 2). It consists of two vertical sheets of perspex held about one centimetre apart in a suitable wooden frame. Several horizontal rows of holes are bored through both sheets so that pairs of matchsticks inserted through the holes will support nuts. As soon as one or other of the two sticks supporting a nut is pulled out, the nut drops to the layer below and finally into the tray at the bottom where it is available. In order to initiate birds a single drop can be arranged, but subsequently up to five drops to successive layers with four nuts on the top row can be set with each test. In one series of thirty carefully recorded tests, coal tits and blue tits were far more successful than great tits or marsh tits. Great tits showed considerable expertise in robbing other tits of their nuts!

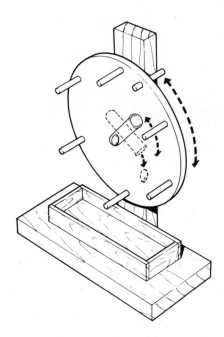

Figure 2

The revolving-disc test consists of a freely revolving disc with peripheral perches and a small test-tube fastened across the centre. A nut is inserted when the test-tube is upright. The weight of a bird alighting on the right perch causes the disc to revolve in one direction so that the nut falls out as the test-tube becomes inverted. One advantage is that the bird can clearly see what is happening to the nut. It may take a little time for birds to get used to a perch which gives way when alighting on to it.

Various tests with match-boxes can be devised. One of the simplest is to arrange a flap which can be pulled down to open a match-box attached vertically to an upright board with a suitable perch. This seems a perfectly simple operation, but it involves pulling the flap forwards instead of hammering at it (see Figure 3) in order to obtain the nut N.

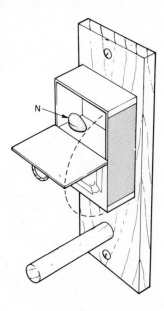

Figure 3

A development of this test with an initiated bird can be envisaged by having two identical boxes perhaps separated by a dividing partition. The bird could be offered what psychologists call the Most Frequent Alternative (the M.F.A.) by placing, in random order, say, seventy per cent of the reward one side and thirty per cent the other side. If possible as many as twenty-five trials should take place in one day and a series of a hundred completed in a week. From what is known of such tests with other creatures, it is possible that after a good many trials the birds will maximize, that is, it will almost invariably go straight to the most frequent alternative even although thirty per cent of the time it will not immediately be rewarded. Very small rewards would have to be used, otherwise the bird would soon get fed up! At the time of writing, this test does not appear to have been carried out with tits.

Another match-box test requires a matchstick to be pulled out from the front of an upright match-box (Figure 4). A weight W then causes the box to drop so as to expose the reward N. A match-box normally fits too tightly for this experiment, so the case must be slit open along one corner and re-joined with cellotape to give slightly more play for the box inside.

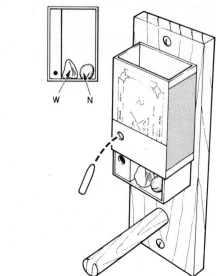

Figure 4

W   N

A third match-box test involves tapping down the box so that a nut falls out of a gap in the front (see Figure 5). As in the previous test the case must be adjusted to give greater ease of movement.

In yet another test the match-box is affixed flat on a horizontal board and the box is opened by pulling it towards the bird (Figure 6). A piece of corrugated paper gives the bird the necessary purchase.

One experimenter got a hen-house sparrow to pull out successive matchsticks and drop a small piece of seed after the manner of the perspex test which was adapted for this purpose. For some reason the cock sparrow failed to compete!

Individual birds show marked differences, even birds of the same species. In the case of a different species much may depend upon aptitude. Birds are usually quick to exploit their successes, but soon give up if no solution presents itself. They do not easily forget what they learn even after long periods. So far little evidence has been produced of learning by imitation. A good deal of entertainment and

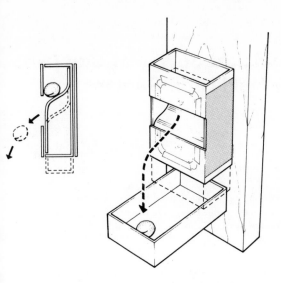

Figure 5 & Figure 6

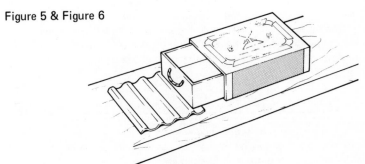

some valuable scientific data can be obtained from these experiments. It seems to be a field in which the amateur can still contribute material valuable in the study of bird psychology.

References

BROOKS-KING, M. and HURRELL, H. G., *Intelligence Tests with Tits* (British Birds, Vol. II, 1958, pp. 514–524).

HURRELL, H. G., *Wildlife Tame but Free*, pp. 165–177 (Newton Abbott, David and Charles, 1968).

Project 32

Ornithological Survey of City Parks, Playing Fields and Gardens

by Colin A. Howes   [S–I–A]

City-bound school children are in many ways at a disadvantage with regard to field work, as the opportunities to study natural habitats at first hand are practically nil. But although perhaps lacking in truly natural areas, cities are by no means devoid of wild life. City parks, gardens and open spaces are great reservoirs of birds and mammals, which can be studied equally well, and with the same methods, as those in the countryside.

In the course of evening or weekend activities, you may visit parks, etc., at some time or other, and whilst doing so you could compile a check-list of birds seen, with notes on numbers and sexes. This will form the basis for an interesting and valuable census.

Graphs and histograms could be produced showing seasonal changes in populations of, say, the rock, song-thrush, starling, greenfinch, etc., whether there are more female than male blackbirds in the parks at certain times of the year, and so on.

Fluctuations in the sizes of roosting flocks of gulls on playing field areas could be studied; also influxes of winter migrants such as field-fares, redwings and waxwings could be recorded in histogram form.

To investigate the preference of various species for various habitats, observations along a line transect across the park could be made, listing the species and numbers of birds in each habitat, the results being recorded as a histogram.

Note: Census techniques as outlined in Project 33 can be used in parks and gardens by more senior pupils.

Project 33

A Farmland Bird Census

by Kenneth Williamson   [I–A]

What is the density of breeding birds in your part of the countryside? How many different species are there? Do some species compete with others for feeding-ground and nesting-sites? With what particular features of the environment—hedges, streams, copses, ponds—is each species associated? If hedgerows and trees are being cut down to make larger fields, how is this affecting the birds?

A 'Common Birds Census', carried out by mapping bird activities on ten or a dozen 'discovery visits' to a sample plot during the course of the breeding season, will enable you to find the answers to most of these questions—though you may have to continue the project over successive years to learn the answer to the last one! A project of this kind is topical and useful: the results help us to understand what birds want from their environment, and therefore assist us in making plans to keep the best possible assortment and numbers of birds in a changing countryside. A continuing census of a sample plot is a contribution to nature conservation, and can be fitted into the nation-wide 'Common Birds Census' scheme organized by the British Trust for Ornithology.

Before starting a census you need to know, by sight and song, at least the commoner birds (you will learn about the scarcer ones very quickly as you go along), and some knowledge of trees and flowering plants is also useful. Choose your plot carefully: it should be characteristic of the local countryside, but not more than about ten per cent of it should be occupied by woodland, orchard or gardens. Include a stream and some pools if you can—indeed, the more varied the area, the greater the variety of birds it will have. Between 180 and 200 acres is about the right size for a farmland plot, and it needs to have well-defined boundaries, such as roads, lanes, a railway-line or canal. (Avoid a wood-edge, or suburban gardens, if you can.)

Having chosen your plot, ask the farmer or landowner if he will allow you to walk round his fields (keeping close to the hedges so as to avoid damaging the crops) to carry out the census. If he says yes, then the next step is to get a large-scale map of the farm and make a tracing of the census plot (e.g. Figure 7). The Ordnance Survey 25 in = 1 mile (scale 1:2500) is the best available, and sometimes the local or county library has copies. If this is to be an official school project, however, you should get in touch with the Populations Research Officer, the British Trust for Ornithology, Beech Grove, Tring, Hertfordshire, and ask if the census can be admitted to the national scheme. The B.T.O. will then help in procuring the maps and producing the copies for the field-work, and will gladly give you any advice you may need.

When you have the map copies, take one into the field on each of your census visits, which should be at weekly or ten-days' intervals from the end of March to the end of June or early July. Enter on the map, as precisely as you can, any bird you hear singing or calling, or see carrying nesting material or food for its young, or performing any other activity of a territorial nature. Any nests you may find should be entered too. There is a special code for each of these activities, and standard abbreviations for the names of the different species, and a list of these can be had from the B.T.O., together with more detailed information about the census than can be given here.

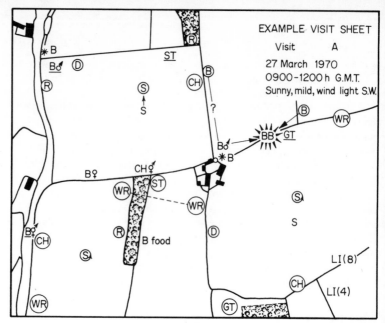

EXAMPLE VISIT SHEET

Visit   A

27 March 1970
0900-1200 h G.M.T.
Sunny, mild, wind light S.W.

Figure 7

Key to symbols in Figure 7

B	blackbird sight record: B♂ female, B♀ male.	Ⓑ—Ⓑ	singing birds seen to take up a new position.
Ⓑ B♂	singing male blackbird. male and females making alarm call.	Ⓑ-?-Ⓑ CH	thought to be same bird but not certain. chaffinch.
B food	seen with food in mouth.	WR	wren.
B*	blackbird nest.	R	robin.
⚡BB⚡	two males fighting.	LI ST	linnet. starling.
Ⓑ---Ⓑ	different birds in song at same time.	S GT	swallow. great tit.

   Letter your 'discovery maps' A, B, C, D, etc., in chronological order, and on each one indicate the date, the time of the survey, how fully you covered the area, and what the weather was like. (Always wait for a fine day if you can, and remember that the best times for bird-song are morning and evening.) When you have completed your full series of visits you will want to prepare separate maps for each species, showing where the individual territories are. To do this for (say), Chaffinch, work through your 'discovery maps' and transfer all the information you have on Chaffinches to a clean map (taking care to tick or otherwise cancel each entry as you transfer it), using the accepted code of symbols, except that, instead of writing CH for Chaffinch (as you did on the 'discovery maps'), you now identify each entry with A, B, or whatever is the appropriate visit letter.

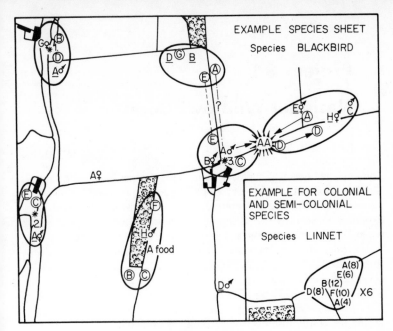

EXAMPLE SPECIES SHEET

Species   BLACKBIRD

EXAMPLE FOR COLONIAL
AND SEMI-COLONIAL
SPECIES

Species   LINNET

A food

A(8)
E(6)
B(12)
D(8) F(10) X6
A(4)

Figure 8

When you have done this for CH Chaffinch, WR Wren, ST Song
Thrush and all the others, you will see that on each map certain
symbols tend to cluster together, without any duplication of visit-letters
within each cluster. These groups represent the territories of the
individual birds. Actually the analysis is never quite so straightforward
as this, for there are complications due to differing territorial behaviour,
but the B.T.O. can send you a document which will help towards a
realistic interpretation of your results. No census of this kind can be one
hundred per cent accurate, but careful field-work and analysis will give
a more clear-cut picture of bird numbers and distribution in the area
than can be achieved by any other means.

With the final maps before you, you can count up the territories of
each species (see Figure 8) and determine the densities in pairs per 100
acres, or pairs per 100 hectares (= 1 sq. kilometre). You can also look at
the distribution of territories in relation to the main features of the
environment—hedgerows (with and without trees), copses, patches of
scrub or marshy ground, streams, and so on. During the course of the
season you should keep a separate map specially for recording this
important information, noting on it the different kinds of crops in the
fields, the types of hedgerow dividing them, the position and height and
species of the taller trees, etc. The B.T.O. *Instructions* tell you how to
do this in such a way that the maximum amount of relevant habitat
data can be obtained for the special map. A lot can be learned by
studying the species maps in relation to this 'key', and not a little of
the knowledge gained may be used in nature conservation.

Project 34

National Wildfowl Counts

by D. P. Holmes   [I—A]

The Wildfowl Counts Scheme is nationwide and has been operating throughout Great Britain since 1948. The results are used for many purposes, and students are referred to the book *Wildfowl in Great Britain*, published by H.M.S.O. in 1963, which shows how much worthwhile information has been obtained, and how it is interpreted.

Basically, the scheme consists of making regular monthly counts, by species, of wildfowl on a given lake, reservoir, or estuary. In Devon, cover is at present provided on the estuaries of the Axe, Exe, Teign, Kingsbridge, Plym, Tamar, Tavy, Taw and Torridge, and the Yealm; on Slapton Ley, and on the Tamar Lake (see (a) below). Counts are made during the winter months from September to March.

Schools can help in several ways, as follows:

(a) Individuals or small groups could make regular counts on the set dates (weekends), and their observations can be included in the results sent to Slimbridge. They could cover an area not listed above, or be absorbed into the existing team.

In Devon more counters are at present specially needed on the Upper Teign estuary, Tamar, and the Taw and Torridge.

Swans and cygnets — birds which may form part of a wildfowl count

(*b*) A school could make its own series of regular counts during school hours. Properly spaced, these would provide valuable additions to the existing organization.

(*c*) Senior pupils might wish to undertake a study of wildfowl habits, feeding, breeding, etc., which, whilst not part of the existing counts scheme, could provide useful extra data. Such studies could be arranged with the Wildfowl Trust, through the Counts Organizer.

An important decision governing a choice of project would be whether a school only wishes to take part for a single season, or whether it hopes to continue for several seasons. However, the organizer emphasizes that all information is of value, and short term observations can be very useful indeed.

Forms on which to record observations, explanatory leaflets, and monthly summaries of the trends in national figures are distributed by the County Organizer. Enquire at your local library for his name and address.

As the counts scheme can be tailored to meet individual needs, it is suggested that any school, or individual, willing to help should first write to their County Organizer giving details of proposed area, time, and frequency of visits, age of pupils, approximate numbers, etc., and type of work preferred. He can then ensure that effort is not wasted by duplication, that as rewarding a programme as possible is arranged, and he can provide forms, etc., and any other literature as and when available.

Note: Schools are asked *not* to write direct to the Wildfowl Trust at Slimbridge, because this would only cause confusion.

Project 35

A Study of Birds' Pellets

by Maxwell Knight   **[I—A]**

Search in your area for the site or sites of regular casting of pellets by a particular bird of prey—an owl is by far the easiest to begin with. Roosting and nesting sites will be the easiest to find, but care must be taken to avoid too much disturbance of the bird; collecting should be done in the evening whenever possible after the bird(s) have begun hunting.

Collect all the pellets present, and use these, which will be of widely differing ages, for practice in dissection and identification of the larger bones present.

Thereafter collect all pellets at regular intervals and attempt to establish:

1. The frequency of casting, and variation in size and correlation between these facts.

2. The numbers of small mammals eaten by the owl by reference to the bones present. N.B. Skulls or parts of skulls are the best evidence of separate animals being present; remember only two right lower jaws means that two animals were eaten.

3. The variety of animals—not only mammals—eaten by the owl; and any evidence of deliberate consumption of other material as roughage.

A collection of small bones found in barn owl pellets

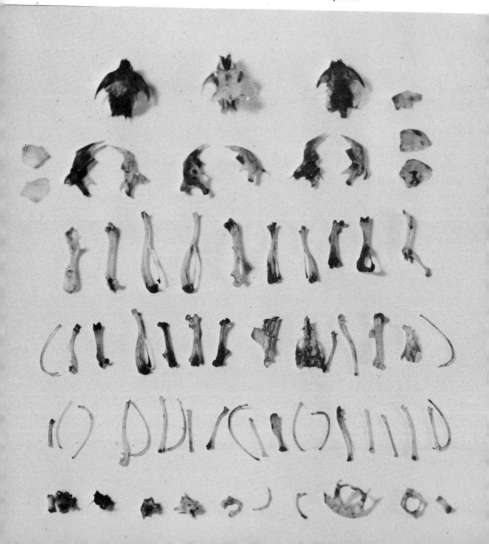

Eventually it should be possible to compare these results with those for other species of owl. Carried out over a number of years it can also give a very reasonable index of the fluctuations in small mammal populations.

Project 36

A Particular Species Survey

by E. A. R. Ennion   [A]

In 1952, 1953 and 1954 at Monkshouse Bird Observatory a 'Bunting Survey', designed to sort out the niches of the three kinds living there,, Yellow, Corn and Reed, was carried out four or five times a year over the same area of about 2.5 km. It showed (among other things) that in the survey area one could expect to find one breeding pair of Yellow-hammers for every quarter of a mile of suitable roadside hedgerow. A few years later, after toxic seed dressings had come into more general use, the area was surveyed again. Conditions otherwise were much the same, but the Yellowhammer population had dropped (1959) to one pair for each two-mile stretch of roadside hedge—only one pair instead of eight pairs present five years before. Reed Buntings were down to one pair for every previous four; but the status of the Corn Bunting had scarcely changed—the very bird which from its name and love of corn-fields one would expect to have fared worst of all!

A survey like this does not require a team of experts. A limited amount of detailed investigation and of the plant and insect life present will, of course, be necessary; one has never yet known expert help refused in genuine cases. For the most part what one wishes to record are conditions and incidents that any alert and reasonably knowledge-able bird-watcher must see during days spent out-of-doors, though he may well have to discipline himself to write it all down in a notebook *at the time.*

References

Instructions for Observers. Common Bird Census, from British Trust for
    Ornithology, Beechgrove, Tring, Herts.

Project 37

From Bird Lists to Census

by E. A. R. Ennion   [A]

Many school children compile 'Bird Lists', and these may be useful
provided always that they only included birds which have been seen
with certainty; doubtful entries are best left out altogether. However,
a mere list of birds' names is only likely to be of use if it covers birds
seen on a remote island or in some area rarely visited before by bird
watchers. In cases other than special ones like these, carry your lists one
step further.

   Add numbers; how many of each kind of bird you see along a
particular stretch on your way home every day—down a certain lane;
going through a park; or past a large garden; or on a lake. Or record the
numbers of one kind of bird; the numbers of blackbirds see in the park;
of ducks on the lake; of lapwings on the aerodrome; of gulls on the
playing field . . . do they vary throughout the year? Do the numbers of
cocks to hens (in blackbirds) of adults to young birds (in lapwings); do
the several species in mixed flocks (in ducks and gulls) vary or remain
the same? Your list becomes a census that can be compared season by
season; year by year; or with similar records from similar places elsewhere. You will be contributing something to the common store of
knowledge about birds and, in doing so, increasing your own competence
and experience as an observer.

Project 38

A Breeding Bird Census in Woodland

by Kenneth Williamson   [A]

A census of the breeding birds in a woodland habitat is more compli-
cated than on farmland (see Project 33) because of the greater bird
density—especially where there is a considerable shrub-layer—and the
general uniformity of the terrain. This makes it difficult to pin-point
precisely one's own position, let alone the positions of the singing birds,
while the close canopy renders birds and their activities much less conspicuous than in the open countryside.

Song thrush feeding young

Such a census as well worth while, however, since woodland bird communities differ widely according to such characteristics of the environment as the dominant tree species, age of the stems, amount of secondary layer or scrub, and kind of management. Therefore, studies can be devised which involve comparison of woodland of the same tree-species at different ages, or in which different techniques of forest management are being practised. Over a period of years one could introduce nesting-boxes and other artifical nest-sites, and assess the results by means of annual censuses.

It is particularly valuable to have studies of plots which form part of nature reserves or declared 'sites of special scientific interest', since a knowledge of the bird-life and its needs may have to be worked into a management plan which also involves botanical and entomological considerations; and also in Forestry Commission properties, since the Commission is now extremely conscious of the amenity value of its work.

The census should be carried out by the mapping method described in Project 33, and the Populations Research Officer, British Trust for Ornithology, Beech Grove, Tring, Herts., will be glad to help with advice on choice of site and determination of aims, etc., and will assist in the provision of maps. A well-conducted woodland census continuing over several years can be accepted for the 'national index' which measures annual fluctuations in numbers of our commoner birds.

In order to overcome the difficulties inherent in field work arising from the factors mentioned in the first paragraph, it is strongly recommended that a grid of 50 metre intervals should be laid down on the census plot before actual recording begins. A base line should be established along the wood-edge or a lane or ride, with zero points A, B, C, D, etc., at 50 metre intervals. Lines should then be set up at right-angles to these points (using a compass) and the 50 m points numbered A/50, A/100, A/150, etc. Care should be taken to check intermediate spacings along the 150, 250, etc., lines to ensure that the grid is approximately true.

If a permanent grid is required, the tree stems at or nearest the points of intersection should be marked with white paint (a ring encircling the bole, and identification marks on two sides with letters and digits about 23 cm high). If the grid must be removed at the end of the season, then white cards with the identification marks in black water-proof crayon can be tied round the stems at a height of 1.5 or 2 m. Where adjacent points are not visible from one another because of intervening trees or shrubs, the direction of the line should be indicated by tying coloured streamers to the branches—high enough to be beyond the reach of deer.

An ideal size for a woodland census plot is 10 hectares (0.1 km^2).

Note: The mapping method may also be used to census breeding birds in other habitats. A particularly interesting type of area is industrial waste ground such as disused canal tow-paths or closed branch railway-lines, which quickly develop useful scrub. In these cases numbered poles can be set up at 100 metre intervals, and in addition to bird-censusing, the dominant trees, shrubs and field-vegetation can be plotted on the map. (Permission for the Inland Waterways Board or Railway Estates Department is required).

Project 39

Variety of Insects

by W. Brett Hornby   [S]

Everyone knows a butterfly but it is surprising how few realize the
variety of the rest of the insect world. A very instructive collection can
be made of just one insect from each of the natural orders. *Insect
Natural History* by Imms (Collins 'New Naturalist' Series) lists and
describes twenty-two orders.

   Just having to discover where to search for each different type of
insect is useful in itself.

Project 40

Insect Visitors to Flowers

by W. Brett Hornby   [S–I]

Select a common plant, e.g. hog weed, which is visited by insects.
Record the species of insect (catch typical specimens) which visit the

Blue-bottle fly — a common visitor to Log weed

flower. Try to get some idea of frequency, e.g. very few, moderate, large numbers.

Try also to gauge the period of maximum visits of all kinds—(this is difficult for casual observers, but the records of species alone would be interesting).

Note: Make sure that the plant chosen is clearly identifiable; hedgerow umbelliferae are notoriously difficult for children, but they should recognize hog weed and Alexanders as distinct from the others. Help in the identification of insects can usually be obtained from your local museum.

Project 41

Insects, Beetles and Small Animals

by K. W. Dendle   [S–I]

Search for specimens under leaves, stones, logs and in the bark of trees. You will find many insects on flowers, near streams or on leaves. You are studying small things so you must really use your eyes. Try to answer these questions and keep a record of your answers. Do not take more than two of each specimen when carrying them back to the classroom for further study.

General

What is it called?
Where did you find it?
What is its colour or colours?
Was it a solitary find or was it living with others of its own kind?

Body Structure

How big is it? Measure it.
Has it three main parts to its body (head, thorax, abdomen)?
Has it got feelers (antennae)?
Are the antennae short or long?
Can you see its eyes?
Are there any wings?
To which part of the body are they attached?
Are there any markings on the wings?
Are all wings alike?
Draw the animal and colour it.
Draw the wings and colour them.

Legs

Has it legs?
How many legs are there?
Are they long or short?
Study the legs carefully and make a drawing.

Defence

Has it a hard or soft body?
Is the hardness in the form of scales?
What protection has it?
Do you know any of its enemies?

Movement

How does it move on the ground? In the air?
Try to make a diagram to show this movement.
Do you think it moves far?

Food

Try to discover its food (manure, decaying vegetation, etc.).
Where does it find its food?
Does it prefer darkness?

Should it have an interesting life cycle like the butterfly, try to make a study of the full cycle. Try to find eggs for your starting point.

Project 42

A Study of Colour Preference in Bees

by F. J. Taylor Page   [S—I]

This project lends itself to wide variation in its method of application. In its simplest form it requires the construction of batches of very simple artificial flowers.

Cut out a large number of 'petals' about the size of those of a Michaelmas daisy. Colour them with bright poster paint in a variety of colours red, blue, yellow, white, green, black—and sort them out into groups of ten. The material used should be stiff paper or thin card, and a small flange left at the base of each 'petal' will be found to be useful.

By means of these flanges stick five 'petals' around the top of a series of small tubes about 0·5 cm diameter (Figure 9) to produce the appearance of flowers. Bind lengths of stiff copper wire around the glass tubes and bend them to form the supporting stem of each flower. Finally, put a solution of cane sugar, between six per cent and ten per cent, into each glass tube with a pipette.

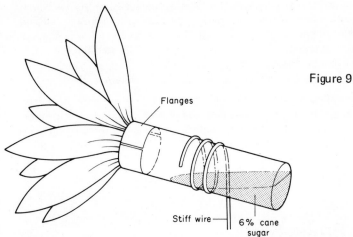

Figure 9

Flanges

Stiff wire

6% cane sugar

On a warm day when bees are flying in good numbers, set up groups of 'flowers' of separate colours near a flower bed. One or more persons can be responsible for a group and should be provided with a small tin of cellulose quick drying paint and a paint brush. Mark each bee visitor with a small spot of paint on its arrival or departure and count the numbers making visits to the 'nectar'. These visits can be timed so that subsequent visits by the same bees can also be noted and the time interval recorded.

Project 43

The Life History of a Cow 'Pat'

by M. J. D'Oyly

[S–I–A]

Aim

To find out what happens to a cow 'pat' from inception to final disintegration.

Method

Observations should start immediately the 'pat' is laid. Beetles of the *Aphodius sp.* and *Staphilinid sp.* arrive in minutes. Note the type and numbers and time of arrival. Later the larger dung beetles take up residence in the base and below the 'pat'. Note the adaptations of the beetles to this mode of existence. Populations of flies and fly larvae are also present, especially dung flies. Record the effect of the 'pat' upon vegetation immediately surrounding it by comparing growth rate and amount of grasses and clovers with the same species a few feet away. Final disintegration is assisted by birds, especially starlings hunting for larvae and beetles.

'Pats' should be marked so that age can be determined.

Notes: This project has the advantage that 'pats' are present all year round and life history varies with the time of year, but identification of species insect present may be difficult. Royal Entomological Society 'Handbook for the Identification of British Insects', is useful in this respect.

Project 44

Woodlice

by W. Brett Hornby   [S–I]

Collect a few woodlice. Refer to *World of Small Animals* by Savory for a key to identification. When the appearance of a woodlouse is familiar to investigators, compile records of numbers of the animals found in various situations.

Woodlouse

Record
  (*a*) Situation (e.g. under stone, in old log, etc.)
  (*b*) Weather (hot/cold; wet/dry; windy/calm)
  (*c*) Numbers of the animals.

Try to decide what situations suit woodlice best. Do they roam abroad more at certain times than at others?

Project 45

Large White Butterfly

by C. V. Antony Adams

The project is divided into three distinct sections, any one of which is likely to yield valuable data provided it is conducted along serious lines of investigation. It cannot be stressed too strongly that the success and value of the project depends upon accurate recording and a large quantity of material being gathered and studied. Several hundred specimens would be a desirable minimum.

Before beginning any section of the project the teacher should familiarize all students with the life-history of the large white butterfly, drawing particular attention to the silk attachments of the pupa, in order that students collecting them will exercise care when cutting through the silk. The parasite *Apanteles glomeratus* should also receive attention, and its life-history be fully explained. Females of this ichneumon may be differentiated from the males by virtue of the small needle-like projection at the tip of the abdomen, the ovipositor.

Section 1

Examine the underside of cabbage and other brassicae leaves for egg clusters. When found, carefully cut away the portion of leaf and place in a numbered tube, recording the necessary note of locality, etc., against the same number in the prepared notebook. The locality may be a garden allotment or field, and a rough indication of the number of cabbages being grown should be given, e.g. about twenty; a hundred; several hundred.

In the school laboratory, a low power microscope should be used for counting the number of eggs in each cluster, the total being carefully noted in the record book against the other details relating to the particular specimen number.

What is the average number of eggs laid in each cluster? Does the large white favour large fields of brassicae to garden plots? How many instances are there of several clusters of eggs being found at one time on a particular plant? What is the maximum number of eggs recorded in a cluster? What is the minimum number of eggs recorded in a cluster?

Section 2

From a given locality collect at least several fully grown larvae of the large white. House them in well ventilated containers, such as aquarium tanks, the bases of which have a layer of dry earth, a few cabbage leaves (replaced daily), plus numerous twigs on which the larvae may pupate. A suitable covering for the tanks may be made from a sheet of perforated zinc.

Of the larvae collected how many fail to pupate due to parasitization by *Apanteles glomeratus*? How many die from other causes? How many successfully pupate?

Collect from the tank the clusters of sulphur-coloured *Apanteles glomeratus* cocoons. Carefully count the number in each cluster and enter this number in a numbered record book. Write the record number on a slip of paper and place it with the cluster of cocoons in a test-tube or similar tube, the mouth of which is plugged with a little cotton-wool. Put the tube in a suitable upright support and deal with the remaining clusters in a similar fashion.

When the ichneumon flies begin to emerge from the cocoons in the various tubes, count the number of males and females in each tube. Enter these details against the number in the record book, together with the date on which emergences took place, then remove the plug and allow the insects to fly to freedom through an open window. Carefully re-plug the tube to guard against escapes by further emerging ichneumons, since not all of them will emerge at the one time. Daily examination of the tubes is essential, as is the correct recording of emerging insects. When no further emergences are noted, count the number of recorded males and females for each tube, and note if the combined totals agree with the total number of cocoons per cluster recorded earlier. If the figure is lower, the difference should be recorded as 'Not Emerged'.

Summarize the total information thus obtained to give number of cocoons per cluster, number of males, number of females, number not emerged. This data should be submitted along with that concerning parasitized larvae as outlined above.

Section 3

From late summer to early Spring of the following year, collect at least 200 to 300 pupae of the large white. These will most often be found under the crossbars of wooden fencing, under window sills and similar situations sheltered from rain. Detach the pupa by cutting through the silk thread on either side of the specimen, and the silk pad at the under-side of the tail. Great care is necessary to avoid puncturing the pupa when cutting the silk pad. In the school laboratory stick the pupae by their undersides to twigs, using 'UHU' adhesive or similar cement.

Note the number of male and female butterflies which emerge each day, keeping an accurate record. The pupae from which no emergences have taken place should be left until the summer when it is possible that further insects will emerge. If this happens, record the number of males and females for each day as before. From the total of males and females calculate how many pupae died. How many, and of which sexes, were the spring emergences and how many emerged in the summer?

Project 46

Leaf Miners

by W. Brett Hornby   [I]

Several fly (*Diptera*) and moth (*Lepidoptera*) larvae find their food supplies between the upper and lower epidermis of leaves. Some of these leaf miners, as they are called, cut out narrow winding galleries, which increase in size as the insects grow. Others eat away irregular blotch-like patches while some start in narrow galleries which eventually spread into blotches.

Although the minute insects which eventually hatch out are so extremely delicate that identification becomes a specialist task, it is interesting to make a collection of mined leaves which can be pressed and mounted.

As a further step which might produce interesting information, allow the larvae to finish their development and finally collect the little insects which emerge. Try to find some link between the type of mine and the insect family.

Project 47

A Study of Solitary Wasps in Semicaptivity

by G. S. Kloet   [I–A]

The study of insects is of major importance today as the ability of the world to feed its ever growing populations must depend upon our better understanding of these creatures and the stoppage of their mass destruction by insecticides, etc. For these creatures are the fertilizers of our fruit—the pollinators that provide us with seeds—the soil makers and the controllers of one another, and every child ought to learn how to study and understand them.

Control of other species is undertaken in many ways, by parasitism, by predation and by the collection, by hunting wasps, of insects upon which to feed their young. The latter presents an interesting subject for study. This project is based upon an observation nest which is simple to make (joinery classes would help here), to erect and to observe, and there is a vast amount of knowledge to be found out about these creatures. The project includes (1) field observation, (2) field experiments, (3) laboratory work, (4) co-ordination of wasp, prey parasites and hyper-parasites, (5) preparation of collections showing opened nests, cell construction, food storage, inter-relationships, etc. All of these are possible with observation nests, and very few have ever been done before. The techniques, stages of research, etc., could be passed on from juniors to seniors as the detail work becomes more complex.

1. The printing department in the schools could prepare all necessary labels.

2. Art classes could be asked to participate and to make accurate sketches of how different wasps carry their prey. Some carry the prey in their jaws, some with their legs. Some use both. Some drag their prey along by an antenna and so forth.

3. Biology classes could experiment by finding the prey (noted by the observers) and capturing female wasps at the observation nests, and placing the two together under bell jars—on some sand —by sunlit windows. In many cases the wasp will paralyze the prey whilst under observation, each species having its own techniques which must be accurately recorded—and published please.

4. Another group can collect all the records of each species and collate these with proper data, making sure that any unusual observation on one insect can be circulated as a 'wanted information' item to all observers of other species.

5. Drawings should also be made of the larva of each species, of the cocoon and how it is made, and of the pupa.

6. Emergence from the pupa can be watched.

7. Larvae and pupae of parasites also want drawing and all collating with the host species.

In this project there is plenty of opportunity for the photographic enthusiasts or artists to illustrate the insects at work—the exposed nests —the 'stinging' of the prey, the emergence from the pupa, the visits of parasites to the nests—the parasite grubs attacking their hosts and a thousand other things never before recorded.

It would be necessary for all the specimens to be properly 'vetted' and at first named by specialists. The entomologists of nearby universities would do this, and once a reference collection is started simplified keys would willingly be provided that should enable students to name the wasps concerned. There are not too many of them—but their prey and parasites are numerous and would need specialist attention until the students learned to recognize them.

The Kloet Observation Nest for Wasps

There are many solitary species of wasps which make their nests in dead tree trunks, old fence posts, rails and woodwork, always choosing sites that face south and each species hunting for its prey and working on its nest only in the strongest sunlight.

They are most industrious, each species specializing in the prey which it catches, upon which it will provide food for its offspring. In order that the 'meat' will be kept fresh, their prey is scientifically paralyzed by the wasp's sting, (harmless to people) which is used with great care to disable the prey by deadening each nerve centre. Thus some insects are stung three, four, five or even more times—each time in a different nerve centre but always the same number of times by the same wasp in the same species of prey.

The prey is then carried by various means to a previously constructed nest in the tree or post and carried into a cell. Sometimes one prey is sufficient to provide enough food for one wasp grub. Sometimes many are needed. The egg is laid on or near the prey and a fresh cell is then stocked. Finally the cells are closed and the wasp starts another nest. When all are completed she dies—her life's work is done. Often these nests are visited by other insects, ichneumon flies and a host of others which are parasitic on the wasp. Their grubs kill the wasp grubs and feed on the prey instead.

Whilst scientists know some of the things that go on inside the nest, many things remain a mystery, as the tree trunks are so hard to dismantle without injuring the insects inside.

Therefore an observation nest has been designed to facilitate the study of these interesting creatures. It consists of a number of small individual pieces of wood—Each about 17·5 cm in diameter—cut from logs taken from different types of trees. These should be about 7·5—10 cm long. Each piece is then split lengthways as shown in Figure 10, after which it is carefully reassembled by means of two twisted wires.

It is now most important that the piece be numbered and the species of wood and size entered on a card index.

Next a cap is made (see Figure 10) to fit a length of plastic or metal guttering that must be let into the ground so that (a) the hollow faces south in a sunny position and (b) it leans very slightly backward so that blocks will not fall out.

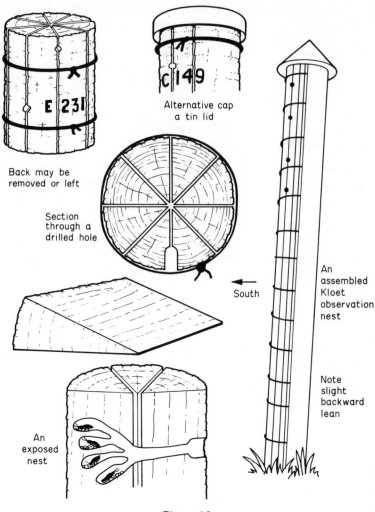

Back may be
removed or left

Section
through a
drilled hole

Alternative cap
a tin lid

South ←

An
assembled
Kloet
observation
nest

Note
slight
backward
lean

An
exposed
nest

Figure 10

Each block is next drilled in one or two places with holes that follow
the splits of wood and are parallel with the top of the block, 12 cm in
depth, they should be of various sizes from, say, 1.5—3 cm in diameter.
These blocks are then stacked up—one on another snugly fitted into
the guttering and copped with a cap to keep out the rain. All holes must
face outwards and the nest is ready for use.

Insects will rapidly adopt these nests and will excavate them, stock
and deposit their eggs in them.

To study any insect arriving with prey, the watcher need only stick
a matchstick in the hole (after seeing the wasp depart); when it returns

it will be unable to enter. It can then be examined through a lens, its prey examined, etc. When the matchstick is removed it resumes its task.

Carefully prepared experiments such as (1) moving the nest to another position, (2) inverting the nest, (3) replacing the partly made nest with a new one, etc., can be made and findings (which are often surprising) recorded.

As nests are completed the blocks are removed, taken into the laboratory and unwired. The pieces are then separated, and by carefully shaving away the wood the nests can be exposed to view. They must be reassembled after examination to prevent desiccation which is helped by wrapping a band of perforated cellotape round the wood. Each piece is then kept in a jar of suitable size and watched from time to time. Other pieces are left in the post to attract parasites and later examined as above.

Here lies enormous work—all within the scope of children. Further information and advice can be obtained from:

G. S. Kloet, 4 Devonshire Park Road, Davenport, Stockport, Cheshire.

Project 48

The Differences between Insects and Arachnids

by D. W. Mackie   [I–A]

Aims

To distinguish the main difference in the structure of (*a*) and insect, (*b*) a spider and (*c*) a harvestman.

Methods

Collect examples of all three groups in the field in suitable corked tubes. Specimens can also be trapped by leaving paper egg cartons (small half-dozen type) upside down in grass overnight and the animals found sheltering there collected next day.

Recording

Write down the following details of each specimen:

Number of body divisions. (Insects—3; Spider—2; Harvestman—1).
Wings or wing cases. (A few insects do not have wings, most do. Spiders and harvestmen have no wings.)

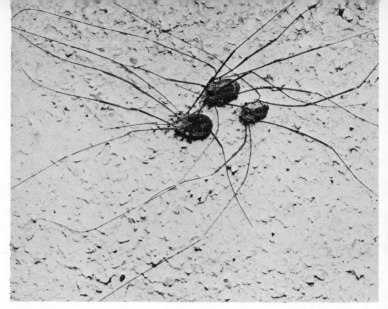

Harvestmen

Number of eyes. (Insects—2 compound eyes; Spiders—6 or 8 simple eyes; Harvestman—2 simple eyes, usually raised on eye turret).
Number of legs. (Insect—6; Spider—8; Harvestmen—8 very long)
Antennae or feelers. (Insects—2; Spiders—2 palps on head, usually short; Harvestmen—2 palps on head, usually long.

Reference

SAVORY, T. H., *The World of Small Animals* (London: University of London Press).

Project 49

A Study of Spiders' Webs

by D. W. Mackie   [I—A]

Aims
To note how many different kinds of web can be seen in a nature walk.

The interesting web of a *Pisaura mirabilis*

To make sketches of each type seen and how they differ in shape and location.

To note how many insects have been caught in each web.

Methods

Seek out orb webs spun on tall plants and shrubs. Note that net web spiders (*Theridiidae*) spin webs on grasses and shrubs and sit upside-down under the main sheet. Note webs of tube-dwelling spiders in house walls (*Ciniflo*) or under stones and bark (*Ciniflo* or *Segestria*). These have radiating web sheets or lines outside holes to catch prey.

Recording

Cages can be made in school to house specimens brought back. Large boxes with glass back and front to house orb-web spinners (*Argiopidae*) or boxes with glass fronts only and a small tube set in end of each box for tube-dwelling spiders. Record all observations on web construction and catching of prey. Note how orb-webs have sticky droplets on web lines to trap prey.

References

. BRISTOWE, W. S., *The World of Spiders* (New Naturalist Series. London: Collins).
SAVORY, T. H., *The Spider's Web* (London: F. Warne & Co., 1952).

Project 50

A Study of Harvestmen

by D. W. Mackie   [I—A]

Aims

1. To find out how many different kinds of harvestmen inhabit a selected piece of ground, such as a small wood or lane with hedges.

2. To plot the different habitats occupied by each species in relation to height above ground level, e.g. leaf-litter, grass roots, plant and grass leaves, tree trunks. This is partly governed by humidity and food preferences.

3. To find out what food will be readily accepted.

Methods

Collect specimens by hand into suitable corked tubes, with notes on each specimen as to habitat, time of day, etc. Examine each specimen with a hand lens to determine markings, eye turrets and details of palps and chelicerae.

Specimens can be kept in glass-topped boxes in the laboratory each with leaf litter on the bottom, water in a small flat dish and a pan of moist earth for egg-laying. Feed them on bread or small pieces of meat, dead insects, etc. Keep notes on all habits observed.

References

SANKEY, J., *How to begin the Study of Harvest Spiders* (leaflet sold by 'Countryside', Hawkeshead, Tower Hill, Dorking).
SAVORY, T. H., *The World of Small Animals* (London, London University Press).

Project 51

Injurious Moth Project

by G. S. Kloet   [A]

Aims

To investigate the feeding capacity of some injurious moth caterpillars. (Need not be confined to injurious ones.)

Method

By breeding a known species from egg to pupa and feeding measured quantities of food.

> Possible species: *Mamestra brassicae* L. —Cabbage Moth
> *Mamestra oleracea* L. —Bright Line Brown Eye
> *Euxoa exclamationis* L.—Heart and Dart.

Females must first be obtained—attraction to light is the easiest method of capture. Place each female in a box and supply portions of the correct food plant for egg laying. Each batch of eggs should be carefully labelled with the date of laying and name of insect.

Each batch should also be provided with a day-to-day date sheet (preferably attached to its box) containing the following headings:

1. Date
2. Number of instar
3. Records of moulting
4. Total weight of larvae batch
5. Quantity of food consumed
6. Average length of larvae.

The most difficult item here to record is the quantity of food eaten. Weight or leaf area are possibilities, but there is plenty of scope for ingenuity in tackling this problem.

Drawings, photographs and descriptions of each instar would add to the interest. (Little information is generally available on these.)

If the work is carried out carefully, it should be possible to produce ratios of food eaten to weight gain of larvae per unit time.

Variation in the emergent imagines from each batch could also be recorded.

Project 52

The Common Blue Butterfly

(*Polyommatus icarus Rott*)

by Alan Kennard   [A]

Aims

To study the life history of the butterfly and make observations in the field on each stage of the insect.

To record the food plants of the larva.

To carry out a marking experiment on a selected colony of the butterfly which will provide data which can be used for suggesting possible factors concerning the colony including:

(a) The overall ratio of males to females.
(b) The ratio of males to females on each day during the flying period of the butterfly.
(c) The average length of life of the butterfly.
(d) Whether there is any substantial movement of the butterfly.
(e) What effect the weather has on the imago (see below).

To rear the butterfly successfully in captivity and produce one or more generations.

To prepare a list of all the flowers visited by the imagines and a note of the colour and scent, if any.

If opportunity arises to identify and note any parasites of the butterfly and also any predators in whatever stage.

Why this Species

The butterfly is widely distributed. It is double brooded, flying in May/June and again in July/August. It may even be triple brooded in favourable seasons and may be seen on the wing almost at any time from May to September. In some areas distinct colonies may be formed which are enclosed in a specific habitat, while in other areas there may not be a distinct colony but the species may occur over a wide area at a small density. The female is quite distinct from the male. The butterfly is readily distinguishable from allied species. For the marking experiment a distinct colony should be selected, if possible.

Theoretical (with reference to aims (e) above)

Consider the following statement:

'The Common Blue butterfly shows a characteristic of an early hatch of males followed by a predominance of females in the latter part of the flying period. When the majority of males are emerging hot sunny weather prevails, thus reducing the average life of those butterflies which are first to emerge. This weather breaks into stormy, wet conditions which drive the butterfly into shelter and a large proportion of the males die, either through the climatic conditions or through predators, with the result that the male population of the colony has been severely reduced before further hot sunny weather induces more emergences which are predominantly of females. There are now few males to pair with the freshly emerged females and the strength of the colony might be impaired.'

From the information that you are able to obtain from your observations could you indicate that any aspect of the above could be supported or disproved? Can you comment at all upon the cover (or shelter) which the butterfly requires when conditions are adverse?

Foodplants of the larva

Bird's-foot trefoil	*Lotus corniculatus*
Rest-harrow	*Ononis arvensis ssp. spinosa*
Black medick	*Medicago lupulina*
Purple clover	*Trifolium pratense*
Dutch clover	*Trifolium repens*
Bird's-foot	*Ornithopus perpusillus*

As noted in Larval Foodplants, Allen 1949
(This list is not exhaustive.)

Reference

SOUTH, R. S., *Butterflies of the British Isles* (London: Warne, 1963).

Marking

Use *cellulose* paint and the point of a fine stick or seeker. Plan your
colour scheme to give you knowledge of day (and place if required) well
in advance. The colour spot can be applied through the mesh of a net on
to the lower surface of the hind wing. If the insect is worked into one
corner of the net first, no damage will result.

This project could be extended to other species of butterflies.

Project 53

The Fauna of Felled Logs—A Group Project

by F. A. Turk   [A]

Felled logs usually have a special fauna, varying in composition in
different woodlands and situations. The study of such a fauna on
different logs can not only be an excellent introduction to the problem
of ecological investigation but can be made to yield results of much
wider relevance, so forming the basis for useful class discussion on
questions such as the humidity factor in the evolution of land faunas.
The subject is a large one and it would seem best to divide it into
different kinds of investigation beginning with a general survey of the
contained fauna and passing later to the investigation of special factors
such as the influence of temperature.

The nest of a leaf-cutter bee established in an elder stump

1. Identify wood of log; note its orientation, e.g. North-South; describe surroundings, e.g. woodland with closed or open canopy; embedded in dead leaves; covered by herbs, etc.

2. Describe state of log; recently felled, wood intact; part-rotten and wet or part-rotten and dry; stripped of bark, etc.

3. Collect all fauna by stripping off bark, breaking up wood with hammer and chisel. Pay special attention to fauna on any fungi that may be growing on the log. Carry out these operations over white paper, and collect animals—including the smallest—by placing them in tubes with a moistened water-colour paint brush.

4. Identify as far as literature and time will allow, leaving the more difficult forms in families. Keep full records of place in or on log, e.g. depth and aspect.

5. Make similar collections from immediately surrounding habitats for comparison, e.g. the underside of stones, dead leaves (by sieving) or herb layers (by sweep net).

6. Prepare tabulations from your records to show, (a) effects of different species of tree, (b) orientation of log, (c) state of log, etc.

7. What tentative conclusions are you able to make? Endeavour to make an hypothesis about the derivation of log-inhabiting fauna from the records which you have made.

8. How far may your results be trusted? Can you suggest any weaknesses in the method and procedure? What other data would it be useful to have?

Among other things which will be apparent from any attempt to think seriously about no. 8 above, will be the need for more precise data

on humidity, temperature, pH values of the logs and degree of rotten-
ness of the wood. (Are you able to think of any way of measuring this
last factor?). Apart from pH values, the easiest of these to investigate is
that of temperature. To take a series of temperatures on different surfaces of logs at the same time, one needs a supply of small thermo-
meters and suitable borers to make holes for these (a gimlet will serve
for fairly rough work). Compare especially the sub-cortical temperatures
of the logs on all sides. It will soon be found that in many woods but
not all (e.g. Norway spruce) the under-bark temperature reached in
full sun in mid-summer is above that which experiment will show to be
lethal to the insects and other arthropods living there. How do they
adapt themselves under these conditions? What influences the temperatures of the logs (degree of conduction of heat around the log)? What
overall effect can temperature have on localizing various species within
the log?

Teachers will find a useful paper to consult in connection with log
temperatures is Graham, S. A., 1920, 'The sub-cortical temperatures of
logs', *18th Report of the State Entomologist of Minnesota,* pp. 26—42.

Make sure there are plenty of dead logs in every degree of rotten-
ness in the wood, before you destroy any, then destroy as few as
possible.

Project 54

The Fauna of Carrion

by F. A. Turk   **[A]**

The dead bodies of animals attract a highly important and rather intri-
cate fauna which, under certain circumstances, may show signs of successive phases in its establishment and dispersal. This is most easily
studied by means of carrion traps. For pleasantness of handling, construct five traps to the following pattern. Into an empty jam jar fit a
nylon net sewn into the form of a funnel, the mouth of which has a
diameter a little larger than the mouth of the jar (Figure 11). Old nylon
stockings, if of not too fine a mesh, will serve well enough. Leave about
two inches free below the apex of the funnel when it is fitted into the
jar. To keep this in place and to keep captures in the net, fit the lid of
the jar on the top and cut a small central hole, about 2 cm in diameter,
in the centre. Bait the bottom of the jars with:

1. A dead mouse or vole
2. A dead shrew

3. A small piece of fish
4. A piece of rancid fat bacon
5. Leave unbaited as a control.

Figure 11

Replace the funnel net and the top on the jars and bury them in soil up to the level of the rim. Over each support, on pegs, a piece of slate or glass about 5 cm above the ground in order to keep out the rain. Endeavour to site the jars at least 23 m apart or whatever is the greatest distance that it is convenient to have them. Examine twice a day making the last visit as late as possible. Collect all the fauna into labelled tubes identify. All beetles must be examined for phoretic mites, i.e. those which 'hitch a lift' on them.

1. What species are taken in each jar?
2. Are there any marked differences between the fauna attracted to the different baits?
3. Can you determine any faunal succession in your records? If so, what causes could you suggest to account for it?
4. Can you identify any known carnivorous species? If so, when do they appear and why?
5. Does the season affect this fauna? If there a difference between those taken in the morning and the evening?

6. Does the degree of decay of the bait affect the species taken in the trap?
7. Can you offer any criticisms of the techniques used and suggest improvements?

Project 55

Plant Galls as a Subject for Class Work, Exemplified by a Project Based on Gall Mites

by F. A. Turk [A]

The gall mites, *Eriophyidae*, are still a comparatively little known group of the *Acari* (mites) and this is especially true of those of Britain. Despite the small size of these organisms (mostly averaging 0.2 mm) they are more easily studied in some ways than other gall makers since, for example, their galls have no true inquilines. Studies on galls—of all kinds—have particular value in connection with school work because they combine the disciplines of zoology and botany. There is scope here too for those students who have artistic ability since the delineation of the anatomical sections of the galls and the mites themselves is highly desirable both as a permanent record for comparative study and in order to stimulate observation. Such studies have been found suitable for a group of not less than four sixth-formers but simpler work along these lines will suggest itself for students of other age groups and attainments. Indeed the whole subject of plant galls is capable of providing a wealth

Oak gall

of work for students of biology and young amateur naturalists, combining as it does simple laboratory work with field study. The best books for the identification of plant galls are in Dutch, but the reference list at the end of this project will be found of great use for all galls and for those of this study particularly.

Preliminary Study of the Biology of the Nail Galls of the Lime

Apparatus

Microscope, flower pots, sheets of plastic, water-colour paint brushes, pocket magnifier, wide-mouthed glass jars. Additionally the stains and usual apparatus of a school laboratory may be useful.

Method

Observe both surfaces of lime tree leaves from early June to September. Count the galls on each of, say, 100 leaves, sampling these, if possible, from different heights of the tree. Do you find any pattern in their distribution? What is the average number per leaf and the frequency range? Do the galls occur on the mid-vein?

Section leaves to cut through one or more galls and mount these in a mixture of glycerine and water. Note the mites inside. Can you distinguish different stages?

Collect living mites by the following method. Put some galled leaves in a closed jar and cover the jar with opaque brown paper, leaving a small slit 2 cm x 0·5 cm. Place the container with the slit towards the light in a north-facing window. After a few days brush the inside of the slit with a damp paint brush and examine the brushings under the microscope until you discover several mites. In this manner collect as many mites as possible from different batches of leaves (note that these should not be more than 2.5 cm deep on the bottoms of the jars).

Collect seedlings of young trees of lime of different ages. Transfer some living mites to a small plastic bag and wrap it around a leafy branch or one of the seedling trees. What happens? Are any leaves eventually galled, and if so, which? What difference is there between those transferred in June and those in September?

What happens to the mites when the leaves fall? Can you follow their movements? Take scrapings from crevices of the bark of a matured tree previously bearing galled leaves. Simmer the scrapings gently in the following solution which can be made up quite cheaply by a chemist.

Rescorcinol	50 g
Diglycolic acid	20 g
Glycerol	25 cm^3
Iodine	Enough to produce a mid-brown colour
Water	About 10 cm^3 or to consistency required

Note: Allow ingredients to dissolve at room temperature.

Any mites will eventually float out, expanded on the surface. Repeat this in late autumn and winter. What forms of mites are to be seen? Where are the eggs? Can you hazard a guess at the simple life cycle of these animals and some of the factors that affect it?

Reference to the works of Connold and Houard will show that there are many more gall mites to be found on a variety of plants, and other schemes for their study will present themselves. Those on the sycamore (*Eriophyes macrochelus* Nalepa and its subspecies *erinea* Trotter) are perhaps the next easiest to work with, as is the mite causing 'big-bud' in the blackcurrant. Transplanting of the mite to other plants of varying age should always be tried. Connold's book will also help if one wishes to study some of the gall-forming insects. The *Cynipids* are perhaps those most suitable for school projects.

SNAILS AND SLUGS

Project 56

Distribution of Snails

by W. Brett Hornby   [S–I]

Collect and mount specimens of shells of snails for exhibition and comparison purposes.

Note dates and exact locations.

Plot finds on maps.

Continue to note locations of further specimens to build up a general picture of as many common species as possible.

Snails can very easily be marked with spots of cellulose paint to investigate the wanderings of individuals.

Project 57

Garden Snail Populations

by Colin A. Howes   [I–A]

This is a simple project which can be carried out either in the school garden or the gardens of the individual pupils.

Aims

To determine the populations of different species of common garden snails, and to discover whether the populations and percentages of each species changed according to the type of garden and plants grown.

Method

1. Make a preliminary survey of the garden(s), listing the crops grown (including surrounding hedges), and work out the area covered by each crop in terms of square metres. Draw a histogram from the results of the survey.

2. In the study area collect a number of snails of as many species as

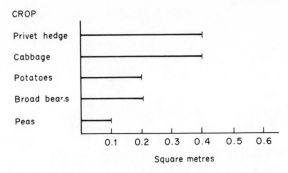

Figure 12

possible. Mark each snail with a spot of cellulose paint, using a different colour for each species.

Next release all specimens back into the study area and leave them to mingle with the rest of the population.

Some hours, or perhaps a day, after release, make a further collection, recording individually for each species (*a*) total number collected (*b*) number of those which are colour marked. From this information, using the Lincoln Index Formula, work out the population for each species.

$$\text{Lincoln Index} = \frac{M \times S}{m}$$

where M = number of colour marked individuals released,
   S = number of snails in sample taken after dispersal,
   m = number of marked animals in sample.

Therefore if ten *Cepea nemoralis* were marked (M = 10) and out of thirty captured after dispersal (S = 30) two were marked (m = 2) the population would be 150.

$$\frac{10 \times 30}{2} = 150$$

If this work is carried out in a large number of gardens with different crops, it may be possible to correlate population variations with the type of plants grown, e.g. some species of snails may abound where the garden is hedged with privet, another species may thrive where bushes of box are grown.

Note: To familiarize pupils with the identity of common snails, specimens can be borrowed from many Natural History Museums.

A common garden snail *Cepea nemoralis*

Project 58

Snail Camouflage Project

by Colin A. Howes   [I–A]

The object of the survey is to determine to what extent the brown lipped snail—*Cepea nemoralis*—is restricted to one particular habitat by its colouration.

Cepea nemoralis has five bands running from behind the lip backwards around the entire shell. These bands may or may not be pigmented; perhaps only one in five is pigmented; perhaps all five or perhaps none at all.

Collect quantities of these snails and make careful notes as to habitat in which found, e.g. tall grass, sward, hawthorn hedge bottom, and note the pigmented bands. In this way you may find that a particular series of band combinations is only successful in one particular habitat.

Visit thrush anvils and collect the broken shells, again noting which bands are pigmented, and thus ascertain which combination of bands is more prone to predation in which habitat.

Once you have found a definite relationship between bandings and the habitat, numbers of unsuccessful variants should be introduced into alien habitats, each snail being given an identification mark (a spot of

paint on the umbilicus so as not to cause the snail to be unnaturally
conspicuous to any potential predator).

Visit thrush anvils in the close vicinty of the released snails regularly,
noting any shells of marked snails and comparing their numbers with
the numbers of unmarked of a different band combination.

Project 59

Conditions Causing Reactivation of Aestivating Snails

by Michael Block   [I–A]

This has been the subject of several investigations, but the results have
been inconclusive. Exact information on the causes of reactivation of
various species of snails could be a valuable contribution to scientific
knowledge.

When snails aestivate they close the mouth of the shell with a film
of dried mucus—the epiphragm—which isolates them from the environment until certain stimuli are strong enough to penetrate to the dia-
pausing animal. If the epiphragm is removed, reactivation is immediate;
but this is not a natural effect. Information is required regarding what
stimuli are effective through the epiphragm and shell.

To obtain standardized aestivating snails, it is best to attach a matchstick to the spire of each shell by means of a blob of plasticine, and to
erect the snails like rows of lamp-posts by inserting the opposite ends
of the matchsticks in holes drilled in a board. Be sure that the animals
cannot stretch out and grip one another, or they will pull themselves
free. *Helix aspersa* needs a good 10 cm all round for safety. Number
the shells with Indian ink, and also their places on the board. The
animals must be well fed and watered at the start, otherwise they
retreat too far into their shells for you to see the epiphragms.

Subject the epiphragmed snails to changes in humidity, changes in
temperature, light and darkness and vibrations (simulating rain). Try
one factor at a time, then combinations of different factors. Keep an
eye on the barometer, as pressure changes sometimes seem to accelerate
or delay reactivation. The epiphragms should be in place for three to
four days before commencing experiments, as the animals do not
become fully deactivated at once. Snails from dry places are good for

this work for six or eight weeks, but small ones from wet habitats will not stand more than a week or two. Release them where you found them before they begin to die off.

Please send the results of your investigations to:

Michael Block, 'Hillcrest', Heads Hill, Crookham Common, Newbury.

Project 60

The Effects of Temperature on Pigmentation of Slugs

by Michael Block   [I–A]

The best slug for this work is the 'milk slug', *Agreiolimax reticulatus*, but other limacid slugs will do. This species is more or less dappled with brown in irregular patches, and appears to be more heavily marked in the winter. It is common in gardens and fields at all times of the year, but a good deal of fruitless effort will be saved by laying slates or planks on the grass in weedy corners. These can be turned over and the slugs examined without disturbing them or their habitat.

Each slug should be recorded as (*a*) unspotted, (*b*) lightly spotted. (*c*) spots covering about fifty per cent of the upper surface, or (*d*) heavily spotted. Records should be made once a month through a whole year, entering on the same sheet the average soil and air temperatures, precipitation, etc., for the month. (A joint effort with the geography department is suggested).

The results can be presented in a variety of ways, and preserved specimens of different colour forms can be exhibited alongside. Most slugs lose their colours when pickled in alcohol, but *A. reticulatus* retains the spots very well. Kill them by drowning in cold boiled water for twenty-four hours, and remember when placing them in alcohol that the bodies contribute a great deal of water to the mixture, so use eighty per cent to ninety per cent alcohol.

For advanced work, several statistical analyses could be made of the data. The work could be combined with other observations such as courtship, growth rates, feeding habits, etc. Check the results experimentally by keeping specimens alive in plastic boxes in a warm room and in the cool compartment of a refrigerator. No ventilation is needed in the boxes, but they could be washed and dried every two or three days. Sliced carrot is the best food. Do not keep more than three or four slugs per box, as they will kill each other. The colours take several weeks to change.

Project 61

Mating, Egglaying, and the Inheritance of Shell-colour in the Strawberry Snail (*Hygromia strilata*)

by Michael Block   [A]

This small snail, common everywhere, has three shell-colour forms; reddish brown, yellowish brown, and white. They are quite easy to breed when kept in plant pots with a couple of inches of soil in the bottom and a handful of *old* dead leaves. Give them a piece of chalk to nibble (natural, not blackboard!), and tie a square of nylon gauze over the top. The food, chiefly porridge oats, is sprinkled on top of the gauze, through which the snails are able to lick it. Stand the pots in a shady place out-doors, and sprinkle them from a watering can if they are likely to get dry.

To obtain virgin snails it is essential to collect them when they are only half grown and rear them in isolation. One snail per 8—10 cm pot is about right. They are mature when the edge of the shell expands into a thickened rim, and can then be paired off in jam jars where they will mate satisfactorily. Equip the jars with soil, etc., as for the pots; jars have the advantage that the eggs are easily seen through the glass, for the snails usually lay their eggs at the side of the jar. When the eggs are laid, remove the parent snails and any food that could decay.

The eggs hatch in about a fortnight, and the young snails stay underground for a few days. When you see the young ones emerge, prepare 25 cm plant pots as before, remove the covers of the jars, and lay them on their sides in the big plant pots so that the young can creep out on their own (they are too delicate to handle). After growing for a month they will need a change of soil, etc., but will then be big enough to scoop out with a spoon.

The life cycle takes about a year to complete, but the colours of the F_1 can be determined in six months. The initial collecting and rearing of virgins can be the work of a fifth form, who can then continue to experiment to the F_2 before their A-level exams. It is advisable to use a snail for more than one experiment, as a single copulation may last the animal for over a year.

Refer to Snail Key in *Land Invertebrates*, by Cloudsley Thompson and John Sankey, Methuen 1961.

TREES, WOODS, AND HEDGEROWS

Project 62

Study of a Tree

by K. W. Dendle   [S—I]

During your studies you should note carefully the changes in the tree selected. DO NOT CLIMB OR DAMAGE THE TREE: When selecting your tree make sure that you are able to reach the lowest branches without climbing. A bank nearby is handy. Try each time to answer these questions. They will help you to write up your notes.

General

What is the outline shape of the tree?
Do the branches stick out at right angles or at some other angle? Draw them.
Try to find out what happens to the wood when it is cut.
Are they spaced evenly?
Do the twigs stick out at right angles or do they twist up or down?
Is the trunk smooth or gnarled (rough)?
Is the trunk a straight one in one piece or does it branch?
Are there other trees of the same kind nearby?
Are there many of them?
Try to estimate the height of your tree.
Measure its girth (around).

Bark

Is the bark smooth or rough? Make a rubbing of it.
What is its colour?
Is it the same colour all the way around?
Is there anything growing on it? If the answer is 'Yes', try to name the things.
If there is a fallen tree of the same kind see if you can obtain a piece of bark.
Measure the thickness. Draw it. Make a plaster cast.

Buds

How are they arranged around the twig (in pairs, singles, etc.)?
Draw a twig with the buds. (Draw a bud, actual size.)

What colour are the buds?
Are they rough, smooth, hairy or sticky?
Are they all alike?
What shape would you say they are?
When do they being to open? (Note the dates.)

Foliage

Is the foliage dense or thin?
What is its general colour? (Light or dark?)
Which way do the leaves face?
Do the leaves overlap a lot, a little, or not at all?

Leaves

Are they simple or compound?
What is their shape and colour?
Are they smooth, shiny or hairy?
Are the upper and lower surfaces alike?
Are the edges smooth or cut?
When do the leaves fall? (Note date that the tree is bare.)

Flowers

Has the tree one or two kinds of flowers?
Are the flowers single or do they form a catkin or an inflorescence?
Are they easy to see?
What is their colour?
Watch carefully and see if they have insects visiting them.
When are the flowers opened? (Note dates.)
When have they all faded? (Date.)

Fruits

Are they simple or compound?
Are they exposed or protected by a case?
Are they juicy or dry?
What is their colour, size and shape?
How are they scattered? (Birds, wind, etc.)
Have they anything to help them to be dispersed?

Sketches

Outline of tree in winter and summer, a twig in winter, flowers on a twig, fruits on a twig, the leaf.

Project 63

Tree Seeds

by W. Brett Hornby   [S—I]

Collect seeds and/or fruits from several common trees: sycamore, beech, horse-chestnut, oak, etc.

Germinate the seeds in a good compost of open texture (loam two parts, coarse sand one part, peat one part).

Make drawings of the seed leaves as soon as they appear.

Allow the seedlings to grow on. Draw the juvenile leaves.

Collect leaves from mature trees to compare.

Notice the great difference in many cases between seedlings and mature leaves.

Common tree seeds (*left*) sycamore, (*centre*) oak, and (*right*) pine

Project 64

Growth Rate

by W. Brett Hornby   [S—I]

Select, say three species of tree common in the area.

By measuring between girdle scars make records of the amount of growth in four or five succeeding years.

Choose twigs from different aspects of the same tree and twigs from trees in obviously different sites: low lying, very exposed, dry situation, very wet situation, etc.

Try to decide how the amount of growth is influenced by aspect and by site.

Project 65

Distribution of Sycamore Seedlings

by R. Wilson   [S–I]

There are various factors which affect the distribution of sycamore seedlings and other seedlings, and this can form the basis of an interesting investigation. It is important that the chosen tree is relatively close to school, so that accurate records can be kept over a period of time.

String or rope should be attached to the tree in the direction of the four main points of the compass, North, South, East and West (see Figure 13).

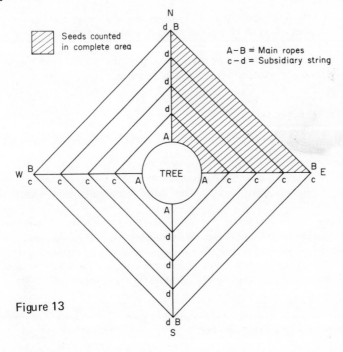

Figure 13

Three alternative studies can be carried out:

(a) Take a strip 30 cm wide, along the length of any radial string (15 cm either side), and note all the seedlings in each 30 cm length. The record sheet below will help in recording the results.

Direction	
Distance from tree (cm)	No. of seedlings
0–30	
30–60	
60–90	
90–120	
120–150	
150–180	
etc.	

The total seedlings for each direction can be worked out, and also the number per square metre.

(b) Attach strings to the main strings, as indicated in the figure, and count all the seedlings within each area of the string grid.

(c) Compare numbers of seeds arriving on the ground with the number of seedlings eventually produced.

Problems

Which direction has the most number of seeds? Why? Compare the number of seedlings and the record sheet over a period of time. Has anything happened? Why might this be? What factors affect the distribution of the seeds?

Does the original number of seeds which you counted represent the total output of the seeds? How are the seeds adapted for dispersal?

Experiments on various 'flight' mechanisms can be made in the laboratory to find out which are the most efficient. This will probably lead to dispersal methods which are used by other seedlings.

Note: There is an obvious correlation in some of this work with the school weather station records.

Project 66

Growing Trees and Shrubs from Seed

[S—I—A]

Introduction

In many parts of the countryside to-day great numbers of broad-leaf trees are disappearing. This erosion is due mainly to economic farming factors dictating the removal of many miles of hedge bank and the annual mechanical clipping of farm hedges. The enhanced value of agri-cultural land, and thus the necessity to grub up areas of woodland for productive farm crops, and the steady replacement of our native tree species with conifers, are added reasons. This project is intended to encourage planting of trees by schoolchildren.

Nursery beds for pine seedlings on Forestry Commission land — visits to these can be arranged

The Seed

Broad-leaf seeds from the species listed in the Appendix to this chapter can be collected comparatively easily as can fir cones from many coniferous trees. Make sure the seeds are not hollow or infested with grubs and that the endosperm is sound.

Broad-leaved seeds are best sown on collection in the autumn, although they do run the risk of being eaten during the winter by mice. Alternatively they can be stored over the winter in moist sand in polythene bags—holly berries must be stored in wet sand for one year—inspect periodically for rooting in the spring and sow immediately the root radicals appear.

When cones are collected the seeds can be extracted after drying on a window sill, and they should then be stored dry in airtight tins in a cool place until required for sowing in March or April.

All tree and shrub seeds can be collected between September and November, and further seeds could be collected under the trees and shrubs after this period. Pine seed is collected in January.

When collecting seed it is necessary that the parent tree should be the best available, as characters, good or bad, are transmitted to the seed. A healthy parent tree with a straight clean bole should be sought.

Space Needed

Tree growth is slow compared to many garden shrubs and plants, and the development of a tree seedling to the stage when it is large enough to plant out in its permanent location takes from two to five years according to species.

It will be appreciated that the area of ground needed for seedlings will be less than that needed for the young plants when transplanted for the first time and that the area required for each plant will get progressively larger at subsequent transplantings, because each individual plant will need more space.

Seed Beds and Sowing

A normal garden bed with good soil, preferably free of lime, can be used or, alternatively, good soil can be put in boxes or pots. Broad-leaved seeds are best sown into the soil a few inches apart in rows about 5 cm deep. Conifer seeds are best sown in shallow drills made by pressing a lath into the soil one or two times the seed length depth. These should be sprinkled thinly in the drill. In both cases rows should be 15 cm apart.

Water regularly and protect from birds and mice by covering the beds with fine mesh wire-netting. Shade against the very hot sun in dry weather and protect against late frosts by laying light branches across the beds. Pull out weeds before they become too big to disturb the seed and seedlings when removed.

A Seed Bed for Town Schools or Back Yards

When ground is not available for growing trees and bushes, the 'Duneman System', perfected in Germany, is an easy way of making up seed beds even on cement floors.

A box-like structure 90 cm wide and 23 cm high and as long as required is constructed of rough slab wood, old bricks or concrete blocks and filled with well broken down leaf litter. When conifers are grown from seed this litter must consist of some conifer leaf litter. It will otherwise lack the *mycorrhizae* needed for conifers to grow and results will be disappointing.

The bed should be well firmed down and well watered before sowing the seed. Seed sowing instructions as set out above should be followed.

To ensure that the seed bed does not dry out during the summer, give it periodical watering. Transplanting distances, if more Duneman beds are being used, are set out in the next paragraph or, alternatively, the young plants could be planted out in whale-hide pots or smaller wooden boxes, using ordinary soil. These pots or boxes should be kept packed tightly together in 'beds' to facilitate easy watering.

Transplanting

A growth of from 2.5—15 cm according to species can be expected in the first year, and it would be best to transplant the seedlings during the following winter months when there is no frost. Lift the seedlings with a fork and tease the roots apart if the plant roots are entwining together, and replant about 5—8 cm apart in the row in the next section of the seed bed and in rows 23 cm apart, or alternatively in the separate pot or box as previously suggested. Press the soil firmly round the freshly planted seedlings and apply water.

During the following winter the plants should again be transplanted, the distance being 8—15 cm apart in rows 23 cm apart. This should also be done again the next year with the seedlings 15—23 cm apart in the rows, and the rows 23—30 cm apart.

The young plants are grown on in the nursery until they are large enough to plant out in their permanent quarters. This will be when they are between 25 cm and 60 cm high according to species. Remember that different species of trees and shrubs grow at different rates, so that whereas some will be in the nursery beds for as long as five years, others will be able to be transplanted at the end of the second year.

Alternatively, they can be grown to larger sizes in the nursery if required, but it must be remembered that yearly transplanting will still be necessary for them.

The transplanting measurements referred to above are offered as a guide only, as it is obvious that they will vary according to species. A rough rule is to give the young transplant twice as much room as it occupies itself in the row, thus allowing for subsequent annual growth.

The purpose of a number of transplantings is to encourage the young plant to develop and form a good root system by the time it is ready to go out into its permanent quarters.

Planting out in Permanent Quarters

The young trees and shrubs are now ready to plant out, and it is hoped that many schools will have ground available to establish their own nature reserve (no matter how small) in which these plants can be used.

Method of Planting

Any tool capable of digging a hole can be used, and it is not strictly necessary to make a hole larger than the root system of the young tree requires. Take care to plant the tree at its original planted depth and make sure the soil is firmed down when it is planted.

Subsequent Treatment—Weeding and Thinning

Weeding operations will be necessary to ensure that the young trees are not smothered by surrounding growth. This can be achieved either by cutting back the encroaching vegetation with a few slashes of a paring hook or by treading it down by foot if it is grass or sparse bracken. If the competing growth is thick and/or tall bracken, possibly two weedings will have to be done each year, one early, one later; these might have to be continued for a number of years when strong growths of bramble are present.

Never let the tree become smothered, although some competition from weeds is desirable to partially shade the young trees and to encourage them to grow upwards rather than to bush out.

It will be necessary to weed regularly each year until the trees and shrubs have put on enough growth to get above the local competition; then they will fend for themselves and eventually dominate the other growth.

Appendix

Tree and Shrub Species to Grow from Seed

Trees

Oak	Rowan
Sweet-chestnut	Bird cherry
Horse-chestnut*	Birch
Ash	Alder
Sycamore*	Yew
Beech*	Scots pine
Elm	Larch
Holly	

Sallows can be grown from cuttings.

Shrubs

Hawthorn	Alder buckthorn
Elder	Common buckthorn
Hazel	Blackthorn (sloe)
Guelder rose	Spindle

*Of the above species we recommend that Horse-chestnut, Sycamore and Beech
are only grown in small numbers due to their comparatively low conservation
value.

Project 67

A Plan to Create a Woodland Nature Reserve

[S–I–A]

Introduction

A woodland nature reserve can be made in most areas of land, and the
main objective should be to create as many types of habitats as possible
in relation to the area available. Thus, while a site of several acres could
possibly include all the variations listed below, small nature reserves
might consist of only one or two of the variations.

Where trees and shrubs are to be used—and even on the smallest site
there will be room for some, the ultimate species retained should be
predominantly hard woods. It will be seen that a large number of different species of conifers have been included in the initial planting programme, but most of these will be thinned out after they have served
their purpose of providing protection for the more valuable hard woods
and for providing early cover for animals and birds.

Planning the Planting

An easy method of planting a thorough mixture of the species selected
is to mark out a piece of the planting area, 20 m x 20 m, with pegs or
string. This area will take approximately 120 trees (being one-tenth of
an acre), which should be counted out in the proportion suggested in
Appendices 1 and 2 and thoroughly mixed in the bunch before planting.
The trees should be planted 2 m apart at the rate of 1210 to the acre.

It is not essential to get the planting distance exact; plant them
roughly two paces apart from each other and remember that the bulk
of the larch and Douglas fir will be cut out as they start to crowd out

the hardwoods. Also, there will inevitably be casualties amongst most of the species as they grow up.

Introduction of Variation

The following suggestions are offered as variations to be included in the main structure of the reserve or, if the area to be planted is small, may in themselves form the nature reserve itself. Much thought is necessary before the final lay-out is decided, but it will be realized that if any or all of the variations listed, or if any of your own ideas are to be included, provision for them should be made before planting commences. So therefore draw up a rough plan of the area and see how many variations can be included.

Variation No. 1   Group Planting

A variation to totally mixed planting could be to plant some of the species into either groups, drifts, or at the edges of the wood. Elms and beeches would lend themselves to this treatment and limes might be specially placed. The same plan could be used with some of the conifers. Groups of Scots pines or larch that will be left as part of the mature wood, would be most attractive and also valuable as a wind break, especially on the north or east side of the wood. A few bird cherries could be sited at one point together and also a group of poplars could be included. All such species' variations give the maximum value as a mixed habitat. Use as many species listed in Appendix 3 as possible. Individual trees could be specially positioned before the main planting commences.

Variation No. 2.   Open Glades

If the area is large enough, an open glade or two somewhere in the wood would be of value.

These and other variations mentioned below, should be planned at the beginning of the planting project, so that no trees are planted on ground that is to be left open. The area selected should be plainly marked out with pegs. Open glades can be extremely attractive if they are bordered with shrubs and small trees (see Appendix 3). They will attract a great variety of birds, butterflies and insects generally, as well as providing variety to the ground flora.

Make the glades of irregular shape and remember, when planting, to allow for the spread the trees will attain when they are mature. It is quite common for fully grown trees to have a branch spread of 6 m or more from the trunk; therefore allow plenty of space. To this distance must be added a further 3–8 m if shrubs are to be planted as an irregular border or edge to the glade.

An alternative to a glade within the wood and particularly applicable for small areas, is to have the glade on one edge, preferably the southern or western side of the wood. The same principle of planting shrubs should be adopted, scalloping the edge deeply to avoid a hard boundary line. Individual clumps of smaller trees could be introduced to break up the scene. Welcome the bramble and the nettle when they appear—as they inevitably will; these are most valuable additions, supporting, as they do, a rich fauna.

Variation No. 3.   Paths and Rides

These will be required in the wood. Generally paths will develop naturally as the trees grow or at the whim of the owner. They will be all the more attractive if they wander between the trees in a haphazard manner.

Rides or much wider paths, required perhaps for vehicular traffic or to introduce a further variation, can also be part of the larger reserve, although these, unlike the paths, must be planned at planting time, so that unnecessary trees are not planted. Mark out the position of the ride—don't make it straight—and plant the trees so that the ride is from 9–18 m wide. Even if a wide ride is not required for vehicular traffic, such a variation can add enormously to the variety of the habitat and the value of the reserve. Wildlife generally congregates at the edge of woods where the light is greatest, and ideally the wood itself should be bordered with shrubs and small trees. So therefore, if the planting area is large enough, incorporate one ride running, if practical, from north to south with a positive bend or two in it, otherwise it will let in too much cold wind in the winter. Vary the width and vary the species planted on the wood edge. Appendix 3 will help you choose the most useful ones. Don't plant them all along both sides of the ride. Leave a few unplanted areas to grow rough grass and flowers. Indeed, valuable species of wood edge flowers should actually be introduced into these small dells.

Variation No. 4.   Thorn Patch

A patch of thorn undergrowth will be of special value to many species of birds for nesting and roosting, as well as being of value for the insects they harbour and the berries they produce. It will have to be sited in reasonable sunlight and, however large or small, should be a solid block of irregular shape to give the maximum feeling of protection to wildlife.

To encourage robust growth and the formation of an impenetrable mass which will defy trespass, early pruning is recommended. This need only be done in the early years to encourage the thorns to shoot out low on their stems, to interwind with each other and to make strong forks for carrying nests. Such patches of thorn could also be sited on the edge of woods.

Plant either black-thorn (sloe) or thorn quicks, or both.

Variation No. 5.   Pond and Marshy Area

One of the most valuable additions to any reserve is a pond, large or small. This will greatly increase the wildlife attraction to the area and thereby increase the interest.

Two principles should be adopted when designing a pond. One part of it should be bordered by shading shrubs or small trees, especially withy and alder, and part of it should be in full sunlight. Thus fauna and flora requiring both conditions will establish themselves and the pond will be the more valuable.

The depth of the pond is also important and should vary from shallow water near the banks to 2 m or more deep, if possible, in the middle. If a pond lined with Aquacrete is not possible due to expense, alternative methods will have to be used. The problem is, of course, in getting it to hold water; if the subsoil contains enough clay, this should seal the bottom to hold the water, but if it is of a porous nature, some artifical means will have to be used. Esso Butyl or similar sheet material, originally designed for field reservoirs, should be suitable. If a pond is to be made attractive to wildfowl, appropriate water plants will have to be introduced (see Appendix 4).

Wet places, where woodcock and snipe feed, are becoming increasingly rare in the countryside, so if an area of very wet marshy ground somewhere in the reserve could be provided, it would be of the highest value.

There will have to be a supply of water, no matter how small, to keep the marsh wet. If a pond is being established, the outfall from it is the natural place for the marsh. Alternatively, if running water from a stream or ditch goes through the property, it should be easy to channel off a small supply and thus create a marsh area. Failing this, is it possible to pipe—with plastic water pipe—a trickle supply from the nearest source?

The actual making of the bog area should not prove difficult. Reasonably level land will be required, so that the run-off is not too fast. A few shallow cross trenches over the area to hold the water and a low earth ramp around, using the soil from the trenches, will provide the necessary wet conditions and encourage bog plants to establish themselves.

Variation No. 6.   Coppice

An area of coppice and standard in a nature reserve is another valuable variation and can be established by a special planting—at 1.5—2 m spacings—of a mixture of ash, oak, sweet chestnut, sycamore, alder, withy and hazel.

Briefly, coppicing is the practice of cutting most of the young trees down to ground level when they are ten to fifteen years old; this encourages them to regrow by sending out a number of fresh shoots from the cut stools. The trees (standards) selected to grow on to maturity should be left at approximately 5 m spacing and should include a mixture of all tree species present.

The value of this type of controlled habitat is due to the fact that the maximum amount of vegetation, both in the form of regenerated growth from the stools and the ground flora, is provided, encouraging the greatest number of insects and thus animal species to the sites.

Ideally, if, say one acre of ground is planted or existing growth coppiced, this should be divided into four or five roughly equal compartments, each of which should be coppiced on a two-year rotation. The cut material will provide firewood for the house, pea and bean sticks, or wood for rustic fences, etc. If it is not required for any of these purposes, if should be cut in lengths and stacked on the site; these stacks would provide valuable refuge for many species of animals as well as a hibernating place. They would also carry their own population of wood-boring insects and fungi as they slowly rotted down.

The leafy tops of the cut material could be burnt on the site.

The coppice area could be maintained by regularly cutting down the shrub growth every ten to fifteen years as explained above, leaving the standards to grow on to mature trees.

One of the chief values of this type of habitat is that it provides vegetation at three levels: ground flora, shrub layer, and tree foliage, and thus greatly increases the number of species the area can carry.

Variation No. 7.   Group Planting on Existing Scrub Land

If an area of land carrying scrub is to be developed as a nature reserve and tree planting is desired, the best method would be to plant small groups or individual trees, leaving some open spaces as glades.

Any of the trees listed in Appendices 1 and 2 can be chosen for this purpose and individual or small groups of conifers, especially larch and Scots pine, would add variety. The scrub area is most valuable and should not be cleared unless a very large proportion of the whole area is to be utilized.

Note: It is not claimed that all the possible variations have been listed; there are doubtless others which will occur to individual land-owners.

Method of Planning

Planting should take place between the months of October and March.

A Devon mattock, with a slightly curved digger blade one side and a straight cutting blade the other, is a most useful tool for this operation, although an ordinary spade can also be used.

With the cutting end of the digger make two deep vertical cuts in the ground at right-angles to each other. Then turn the digger to use the other blade and pull the cut section back; it will most likely hinge open. Stand the young tree in the *corner* of the removed section and push the lifted sod back into place. Be sure that the tree is not planted too shallow or too deep. Finally stamp the sod back so that the tree is firmly held in an upright position. Planting by this method is quick and cheap.

Subsequent Treatment—Weeding

If, during the summer following planting, it is found that a large number of young trees have died from one cause or another, it is advisable to fill up these gaps with fresh plants. Try to adhere to the same mixture of species.

To ensure that the young trees are not smothered by surrounding growth, weeding operations will be necessary. These can be achieved either by cutting back the encroaching vegetation with a few slashes of a paring hook, or treading it down by foot if it is grass or sparse bracken. If the competing growth is thick and/or tall bracken, possibly two weedings will have to be done each year, one early, one later; this might have to be continued for a number of years, when strong growths or bramble are present. Once the trees have grown above this bramble, the latter can be allowed to form a most useful thicket of their own.

Never let the tree become completely smothered, although some competition from weeds is desirable, partially to shade the young tree and to encourage it to grow upwards, rather than to bush out.

Thinning

After about five or six years of growth, thinning will have to be commenced and this is the creative time of the nature reserve management, when the ultimate distribution of species, one with another, will begin to appear.

The fast-growing conifers—larch and Douglas—will be the first trees needing attention. With some it will be a case of pruning off-side branches, which begin to shade or suppress the more valuable hard woods. One can be quite drastic with the pruning, cutting off all branches for up to half the height of the tree if necessary. Other trees will have to be removed completely; a large number of the conifers will have to be cut down anyway after they have served the main purpose of being a nurse crop for the broad-leaf species; they are in this sense expendable. Unless there are physically strong people to help in the felling and cutting-up work, avoid letting these trees grow too large: take them out when they are easily handled. If there is plenty of help, let as many as possible grow to stake size timber, providing they do not jeopardize the development of the others.

Many individual conifers can be left permanently in the wood where they have room to grow and to give greater variety and, if possible, specimens of *all* the species originally planted should be retained.

As the hard woods grow, progressively prune off the lower side branches of the best specimen trees. There is no reason why some good class timber should not be grown, and this pruning operation will also allow morellight into the wood for the introduction and establishment of a shrub layer and a flourishing ground flora by natural regeneration.

The final density of trees in the wood is up to the individual owner, but a fairly open woodland canopy should ultimately be achieved by progressive thinning during the life-time of the wood.

Appendix 1

Species of hardwoods	Trees to the acre	20 m x 20 m
Oak	300	30
Birch	60	6
Beech	10	1
Ash	60	6
Sycamore	10	1
Hornbeam	50	5
Sweet-chestnut	40	4
Horse-chestnut	10	1
Elm	60	6
Lime	10	1
Willow	50	5
Bird cherry	10	1

Appendix 2

Species of conifers	Trees to the acre	20 m x 20 m
Larch	140	14
Douglas fir	130	13
Scots pine	130	13
Silver fir	40	4
Noble silver fir	60	6
Western hemlock	50	5

Appendix 3

Alder buckthorn	Alder
Bird cherry	Crab apple
Poplar	Birch
Rowan	Holly
Yew	Hazel
Hawthorn	Willow
Guelder rose	Blackthorn (sloe)
Elder	

Note 1: It is, of course, not possible to buy all these species from a commercial nursery; some will have to be grown from seed specially collected or from cuttings.

Note 2: Alder, poplar, willow and withies are especially suitable for damp conditions or by the sides of ponds and streams.

Appendix 4

List of Species of Pond Plants

Pond weeds, species
Branched bur-reed
Water cress, species
Buttercup, species
Amphibious bistort
Pale Persicaria
Stonewort
Orache
Water pepper
Corn spike rush
Common bullrush

Water millfoil, species
Sedges, species
Flote and water grasses
Great water dock
Mare's-tail
Red leg
Water crowfoot
White clover
Clustered dock
Duck weed

Do not plant Canadian water weed, as this tends to choke other submerged plants and is of little or no food value.

For Planting Around the Pond

Birch
Oak
Withy

Alder
Blackberry

Some of the water plants are not in themselves of direct food value to ducks, but provide suitable conditions for the natural appearance of insect species which are eaten by wildfowl.

It is strongly recommended that alien plants are NOT introduced.

It is recommended that water plants are established in the spring of the year to save them from winter storms which might dislodge freshly planted plants.

Project 68

Signs of Feeding Habits in Conifer Woods

by Alfred Leutscher   [I—A]

With a steady increase in forestry over the past fifty years, especially with the planting of conifer plantations, many changes have taken place in the distribution of our fauna. For example, deer and red squirrel have spread and increased as a result, also certain birds such as crossbill and owls.

It is often complained that conifer woods are dull, dark and mono-
tonous places to walk in, and appear largely devoid of wildlife. This
may be true in terms of numbers and species, but on the other hand
such woods often harbour some of our rarer and shyer creatures because
of their remoteness and lack of disturbance by man (e.g. Highlands,
Breckland and Lake District).

A walk through a conifer wood can reveal much in the way of
animal presence, even without seeing a single appearance. Signs of
feeding are left about for anyone to see, such as the following:

1. Cones with their bracts bitten down to the central column, found
   in piles on logs and tree stumps (work of squirrels—keep a look-
   out for the red).
2. Isolated fallen cones with bracts torn or twisted (work of crossbill, a winter visitor in the south).
3. Bark damage. This can vary and is not so easy to identify. Look
   for teeth marks along edges of eaten bark, also height of damage
   above ground. At ground level this could be rabbit. Fallow and
   red deer occasionally gnaw at bark, up to 1.2 m and 1.8 m
   respectively. Above this could be squirrel.
4. Damage to foliage. Buds and leaves which are bitten off cleanly
   rather than torn off, suggest squirrel. Look for tufts of leaves
   from tips of branches lying on ground, either conifer, or deciduous
   such as oak or beech. Squirrels are wasteful feeders. Signs of torn
   branches could mean the work of deer, either from tearing away
   food, or from 'cleaning' or 'thrashing'. The former occurs when
   the antlers are being rubbed clean of velvet, and the latter during
   the excitement of rutting. The soil will also be disturbed. Close
   cropped grass could be rabbit or sheep. Tufts of grass torn away
   suggests deer or cattle.
5. Signs on hard fruits. Many conifer plantations now have a fringe
   or 'amenity' belt along their borders, made up of oak, beech and
   so on. Look out for fallen acorns, hazel nut, hornbeam nutlet and
   beech nut. Ragged holes in acorn and nut could be squirrel. More
   rounded holes could be woodmouse, and very neat, round holes
   especially in hazel nuts, might indicate the presence of the pretty
   dormouse. If its nest is discovered, please *do not disturb.* It still
   occurs in Devon, but is getting rare as a British mammal. Beech
   and hornbeam nuts split in two are the work of birds, probably
   finches. Those with tiny holes in are made by mice and voles.
   Look for a woodmouse's store of food under logs and tree roots,
   in hollow trunks and in old bird's-nests.

References

KNIGHT, M., *The Young Field Naturalist's Guide* (London: G. Bell, 1952).
LEUTSCHER, A., *Tracks and Signs of British Animals* (Basingstoke:
   Macmillan, 1960).
SPEAKMAN, F., *Tracks, Trails and Signs— The Young Naturalists' Year*
   (London: G. Bell, 1954).

Project 69

A Transect Through a Wood to Discover Certain Inter-relationships in the Environment

by J. Whinray, F. Hollinshead, K. Howard   [I–A]

This project is designed so that it can be used for all levels of age and ability throughout a secondary school; the teacher can use it to draw various types of information from pupils, making it more or less involved as he wishes.

The main work involves taking a transect through a suitable wood. (A small wood is best, so that the transect can go right through a wood from north to south). A shaded school field could be used just as easily.

The equipment needed is simple, consisting of:

> 0.5 metre quadrats
> Measuring tapes or chains
> Navigational compass
> Photoelectric exposure meter

It is felt that only one type of dominant plant should be investigated. First study the selected plant, including a brief history, conditions of growth, etc.

Next draw a plan of the wood, including compass bearings, and cross section of the lie of the land.

Measure the population density and height of the selected plant using a ½ metre quadrat and a ruler. Light intensity is simply a comparitive measurement, the dimmest area being called 'unity' and other readings proportional.

Tabulate your results and use them to draw the following graphs:

(a) Average plant height plotted against concentration of plants.
   This will show increases to both north and south. Why was increase to south greater than to north?

(b) Position in wood of plants above and below 20 cm.
   South will have higher percentage of plants greater than 20 cm in height. Why?

(c) Light intensity plotted against average height of plants.
   Does the angle the ground of the wood makes with the sun's rays have any affect on density or height?

(d) Form an overall picture which will show that density of plant population increases towards the edge of the wood. Why? No plants will be found around the boles of larch trees. Why?

All the unanswered questions provide a wealth of material for further work both in the library and in the field. Along with those questions, pose the following:

What effect do the following factors have upon height and density of plant population?

1. Wind, rainfall, temperature.
2. Soil conditions.
3. Drainage of the slope.
4. Conditions of surface of the earth.

Is the method of measuring light a valid one?

Project 70

Study of an Individual Tree

by R. J. Revell   [I–A]

Aims

1. To study the structure and life history of a single tree, and record the changes which take place during a period of one year or more.

2. To investigate the animals and plants living upon, or in close association with this tree.

3. To compare 1 and 2 above for several individual trees of the same species growing in differing situations.

Notes

1. A large isolated tree is best. Its exact position, situation with regard to other trees and buildings, and degree of exposure should be recorded.
    Record height and girth at several levels, spread of shoot system, spread of root system, estimated age, etc.
    Record dates of bud burst, flowering seed or fruit dispersal, leaf fall.
    Record growth in length of shoots in different parts of tree.
    Make measurements and drawings to show range of leaf shapes and sizes. (Further work could be done to ascertain stomatal index, estimate of total leaf area, etc.)
    Draw the structure of flower and pollination mechanism (per cent fertility of pollen, pollen germination time).
    Draw the method of seed or fruit dispersal (per cent fertility for that

particular year could be estimated by careful work).

Study the per cent germination of seeds and method of germination.

2. Record epiphytic and parasitic plants to be found on the tree (much detailed study could be done here on aspect, extent and height above ground of each species).

    By searching and beating, investigate the invertebrate fauna at (say) four set times during the year. Eggs, larvae and pupae could be bred out for identification purposes.

    Record mammals and birds associated with the trees at various times of the year. Nesting dates, types of food, etc.

    Record all galls to be found on the tree.

    Support the records with drawings and/or photographs.

Difficulties

The greatest difficulty lies in the identification of plants and animals associated with the tree.

Ferns are easy to identify, and mosses are reasonably easy (except *Ulota* and *Orthothecium*). For lichens the 'Observer' book is very good, and for fungi there are several good new books on 'macros'; 'micros' are almost impossible to identify.

There are keys available for most invertebrates likely to be found in trees but these are difficult to use. 'Wayside and Woodland' series useful here, and Collins New Naturalist Book, *Insect Natural History*.

Dangers

Indiscriminate beating must be avoided. Some climbing is almost essential.

Project 71

Hedgerow Projects for Schools

by Max Hooper   [I—A]

Introduction

The aim of this project is two-fold: first to help teachers introduce field studies into their courses and link such studies with classroom subjects such as history and second, to provide information of use to the Nature Conservancy.

The Nature Conservancy administers nearly a quarter of a million acres of National Nature Reserves in Britain. This sounds an impressive figure but only one-fifth of this acreage is in England; four-fifths of the total area is in mountainous areas, particularly in Scotland and Wales. Also the natural vegetation of Britain is woodland but only four per cent of the Reserve acreage is woodland. To redress the balance more woodland wildlife should be preserved. At the moment the situation is not quite as serious as it may sound simply because so much of our land is hedged. Hedges are in a great number of facets very similar to that most rich of woodland habitats, the woodland edge. To hedges, for example we owe the fact that our woodland birds can survive so well in agricultural land. Hedges are most common in lowland areas and the most recent estimate of their acreage suggests that they cover nearly twice the acreage of our Nature Reserves. In addition, access to Nature Reserves is limited to prevent undue disturbance by man and they are therefore very seldom available for teaching projects with large classes.

Hence since there is a greater acreage of hedgerows than reserves, and hedges support a large proportion of our lowland wildlife and further are more accessible than reserves, their ecology should be studied more thoroughly. The situation is urgent because modern agriculture requires larger fields and many hedges have been grubbed up.

Hedgerow Survey

As a beginning in the investigation of hedgerow ecology we are trying to survey the distribution of different types of hedgerow, their management and the kinds of shrub in them throughout the country. This information is recorded on the proforma shown below.

The technique of filling in the proformas is to select a hedge and record on the proforma all the features present in a 30 m length of that hedge.

When a sufficiently large number of hedges has been recorded the results will be analysed by computer.

We ask that anyone who is interested should examine as many hedges as possible and send in a proforma for each one. In this stage of the investigation even incomplete information is useful and no one should be deterred because they cannot determine the age of the hedge or define the soil type.

School Project

Through the courtesy of the Wildlife Youth Service a number of proformas reached schoolchildren, were filled in and returned most successfully. As yet, however, we have only an incomplete picture of the hedges of the country as a whole and we would welcome more proformas from all areas.

To fill in proformas alone is a great help to us but, apart from being an introduction to systematic recording, this is probably not of itself of much use in education.

HEDGEROW PROJECT   RECORD SHEET

Name of Recorder . . . .   Date . . . .

County . . . .   Grid Reference . . . . .

Locality . . . .

Age of hedge (if known)	Shrubs and trees present
Parish boundary hedge	in the 30 m length of
Not a parish boundary hedge	hedge chosen. Please
	ring all those species
	present.

Pure hedge—one kind of shrub   Ash
   predominant   Beech
Mixed hedge—several kinds of shrub   Blackthorn
   equally predominant   Crab apple
Managed by clipping   Elder
Managed by layering   Elm
Not managed recently   Field maple
                                       Hawthorn
Trees present   Hazel
Trees absent   Holly
                                       Oak
Soil: clay   Privet
Soil: sand or gravel   Rose
Soil: chalk or limestone   Sycamore
                                       Willow

                                                   Please write in below the
                                                   names of any other
Add further comments below: species.

Return to M. D. Hooper, Monks Wood Experimental Station,
Abbots Ripton, Huntingdon.

However, our preliminary results indicate that:

(a) the number and variety of birds' nests in a hedge depend in part
     upon the management of the hedge and in part upon the number
     of kinds of shrubs present in the hedge,

(b) the number of kinds of shrub in a 30 m length of hedge depends in part upon the management of the hedge, in part upon the type of soil in which the hedge is growing and to a very large extent upon time during which the hedge has been in existence. In general a hedge 100 years old has only one or two species of shrub, a hedge 200 years old has 2 or 3 species and so on until a hedge 1000 years old has 10 or 12 species.

Hence it should be possible to link geographical, geological, biological and historical studies.

The manner in which this is done will of course depend upon local circumstances, most particularly upon a teacher's own interests, and the following project is no more than a suggestion.

For a simple exercise you could compare the number of shrubs in 30 m of a parish boundary hedge with the number of shrubs in an adjacent hedge. The parish boundary hedge one might expect to be about 1000 years old and therefore have about 10 different kinds of shrub in it. The adjacent hedge may be no more than 200 years old and have only two species of shrub in it. From this observation it is possible to go in either of two directions and ask why is one hedge rich and the other poor in species or, alternatively, ask what consequences will this difference have on the animals living in the hedge? Simple hypotheses may be set up and tested in various ways. For example, one might suggest that because there are a greater number of kinds of plant in one hedge, there should be a greater number of kinds of insects and this could be tested by using jam jars as pitfall traps for beetles or by counting the number of butterflies along the hedge. Or one might suggest that because a hedge has been in existence a long time there has been a greater chance for seeds of other shrubs to be brought in by wind or by birds. Most shrubs have fleshy fruits which are eaten by birds so one could perhaps go on to examine the soil under, say, starling roosts for seeds. Or one could argue that if a hedge 1000 years old has 10 kinds of shrub and one which is 200 years old has two kinds, then one 500 years old should have five, and then search for hedges with five kinds of shrub and try to find out how old they are.

Possibly the most rewarding form of the project would be for a rural school over a period of time to build up a complete history, biology, geography and geology of the hedges in their own parish. (The opportunities for this are to some extent limited by the availability of the historical material and a brief appendix has been added showing some of the most likely sources.)

The biology would be the lists of plants, and, say, birds and butterflies in the hedges surveyed by the children themselves and the geography and geology can be taken from the modern ordnance survey maps.

The results could take two forms: a set of completed proformas which would be most useful to us and a set of maps showing the geology and geography of the parish, the age of the hedges (old hedges in red, young in blue, etc.), the flora of the hedges (rich hedges in red, poor in blue, etc.), the birds' nests (blackbird nests ringed, skylarks with crosses, etc.) which should make excellent wall charts for a classroom and be ideal demonstration material for school Open Days.

The main points are, however, that the Nature Conservancy should get a large number of hedge records and that a host of questions should arise and be answered by the children's own efforts:

Hedge A has more birds than Hedge B. Why? Is Hedge A richer in shrubs; if it is, is it older or is it not so well managed? If it is older, when was it planted, is it part of a Tudor enclosure for sheep which was later sub-divided? When and why was it sub-divided? Was it the price of corn in the Napoleonic Wars? Why should that area be used for sheep, is it a lighter, poorer soil only fit for grass or was it so far from the village as to make ploughing with oxen and horses time-consuming because of the long trek morning and night to the area and back?

Historical Sources for Dating Hedges

The earliest source is likely to be a boundary clause in an Anglo-Saxon Charter. These survive for only a few parishes and can be extremely difficult to interpret. Possibly the best introductions are *The Early Charters of Eastern England* by C. R. Hart and *The Early Charters of the West Midlands* by H. P. R. Finberg, both published by Leicester University Press.

Details of the history of land use between 1066 and the middle of the sixteenth century are often very difficult to find. The most useful summary is usually to be found in the relevant volume of the *Victoria County History.* From the end of the sixteenth century, the use of maps becomes more common and most County Record Offices have excellent collections of estate maps; the County Archivist should be consulted as to their use and interpretation.

In most cases, it sould be possible to go back at least 100 years to either an Enclosure Award Map or a Tithe Map.

The Tithe Map, which if it exists should date from the period 1840 to 1880, can sometimes be consulted in the parish, as a copy should be deposited with the person and another copy with the diocesan records. Many of these have been lost over the years but The Tithe Redemption Office (Barrington Road, Worthing, Sussex) has copies of all the Tithe Maps made and will provide a photostat copy.

Sometimes the tithe was extinguished at the time of enclosure and hence no Tithe Map will exist so that one must trust to finding an Enclosure Award Map. Most of these date from the period 1760–1820, though there are a few both earlier and later and these can usually be found in the County Record Office, although in some cases a copy may be found among the church records.

Early Ordnance Survey Maps of the larger scales should also be con-sulted where possible. These may be found in the County Record

Office or the County Library. The most recent 2½ in. or 6 in. Ordnance
Survey Maps together with the 1 in. geological map of the area chosen
should be purchased. Possible additional sources for more recent changes
are the maps of the Land Utilization Survey published just before the
1939–45 war and aerial photographs. For most areas of England, the
Air Photographs Library of the Ministry of Housing and Local Govern-
ment (Whitehall, London, S.W.1.) has photographs of various dates from
1946 onwards and will provide prints at a price of 30 p each, which is
reduced to 17½ p for staff and students of educational establishments.

Copies of the proforma may be obtained from and should be returned
to:

Dr. Max Hooper, The Nature Conservancy, Monks Wood
Experimental Station, Abbots Ripton, Huntingdon.

References

MEIKLE, R. D., *British Trees and Shrubs* (New Series, London, Eyre and
    Spottiswoode, 1958).
SOUTH, R., *The Butterflies of the British Isles* (Wayside and Woodland Series,
    London, Warne, 1953).
VEDEL, N. and LANGE, J., *Trees and Bushes in Wood and Hedgerow,* (London,
    Methuen, 1960).

PLANTS OTHER THAN TREES

Project 72

Study of a Flowering Plant

by K. W. Dendle   [S]

During your visits to a particular habitat you should revisit the plants
under study to note any changes in them. Changes in how open the
flowers are, the brightness of the petals, the fall of the petals, etc. When
removing a single plant *do not disturb too much soil.* Take care with the
trowel to remove the roots undamaged. Preserve your specimen carefully. Try to answer these questions. Keep a record of your answers.

General

What is the size of the plant? Measure its height.
Where was it found? (Wood, river bank, hedgerow, etc.)
Where there many similar plants?
Can you identify any of the neighbouring plants?
Draw a plan of the site (one yard square) and colour the various plants.
Which way does the site face? (Point of compass.)
Is it exposed or sheltered?

Wild bluebells

Roots

Does the plant have a tap or fibrous root system?
Measure the length.
Does the plant grow from a bulb?
Examine the roots under the magnifying glass. Can you see the root hairs?
Draw the root system and colour it.

Stalk

What is the shape of the stalk? Cut across the stalk to find out (round, oval, square).
Is it a climbing plant?
Is the stalk smooth or hairy?
Is it strong or weak?
Does it bend easily or does it snap?

Leaves

Are the leaves simple or compound?
What is the shape of the leaf?
Is it rough, smooth or hairy?
Are the upper edges cut or smooth?
How are the leaves arranged around the stalk?
Has the leaf a leaf stalk?
Draw several leaves and colour them.
Where are the largest leaves found?

Flowers

What is their colour?
How many petals are there to each flower?
Are the petals separate or joined?
What is the shape of the flower?
Have you seen any insects visiting the flower?
Can you easily see the stamen?
Draw the flower and colour it.

Seeds

Where do the seeds form?
What colour are they?
Are there very many of them?
How do you think that they are dispersed?
Collect some and try to grow seedlings next year.
Keep the seeds in bags that are labelled.

Press two flowers and two leaves for your collection. Make a rubbing of a leaf. Do not try to study too many plants.

Project 73

An Investigation of the Distribution of the Plants in a Lawn

by F. J. Taylor Page   [S—I]

A study of a lawn or field requires that you should not only know the names of the plants that are to be found there, but also how many of each species exist. This is a class project, but it is a good idea for each one of you to make sure first of all that he knows the plants on a lawn and can recognize them by their leaves. To do this each of you make your own collection of leaves, draw each type in a notebook, and with the help of your teacher or a book name each drawing.

The next step is to lay out a large square with string. Everyone should make a sketch to show the patches mainly occupied by each kind of plant that can be identified.   An example is shown in Figure 14.

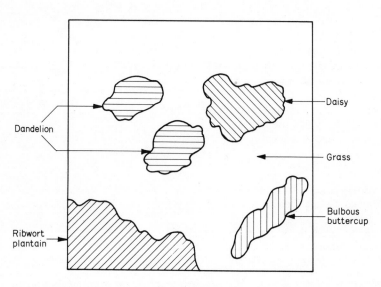

Figure 14

This emphasizes that there is a variation in distribution. A number of smaller squares constructed by smaller groups will emphasize this still further.

To compare the frequency of each species of plant, the class lines up at one end of the study area, and each person marks the heels of his or her shoes with a chalk mark. Two people then stretch a string across the area 5 metres ahead of the line. Each member of the class now steps out until the string is just about to be crossed and records the name of the plant which is touched by the chalk mark. This is repeated by moving the string another 5 metres ahead, and again the class moves up and records the plants touched by the chalk mark. In this way, steadily moving forward and recording, the class as a whole is surveying not only the frequency of each species over the whole area, but also changes in frequency that exist between the upper and lower ends of the study area.

Once all the records have been made individually they are added up, the total records of each species being made for each 5-metre forward progress, and also the total for each species over the whole area. The construction of graphs produces interesting information concerning the relative frequency of each species and the change of frequency, particularly if the area chosen is sloping or there are significant areas of light and shade or where trampling and non-trampling occurs.

Project 74

Weed Seeds and Seedlings

by W. Brett Hornby   [S—I]

Collect and carefully label seeds of a number of common weeds, storing them in suitable envelopes ready for examination. If possible use a good lens to examine them—make drawings.

Attempt to germinate a number of seeds immediately. Record percentage of success.

Keep samples and attempt germination the following year. Compare percentage of success.

Make drawings of seedling stages of successfully germinated seeds. Record whether cotyledons remain in the ground or are raised above the ground.

Project 75

Climbing by Twining

by W. Brett Hornby   [S–I]

Find out whether stems of plants which climb by twining can use all
supports no matter how thick or thin.

This is an experiment to carry out in the garden. Use runner beans.
Arrange a series of possible supports; a single wire for the thinnest then
a range of sticks or posts with up to four seeds to each support. As the
growth proceeds decide whether the twining stems make easier use of
some posts than others. At the same time decide whether all the stems
twist in the same direction.

Tie one or two stems so that they are forced into the opposite twist.
What happens later?

Project 76

Leaf Polymorphism

by W. Brett Hornby   [S–I]

Collect leaf specimens from plants which show a variety of leaf shape.
Ivy is a good one to begin with.

By any suitable means—rubbings, spray paint from toothbrush, etc.—
make records of the outline shape of the leaves. Arrange these outlines
to show graduations in general outline—if possible relate shape to
position on plant, or growing site, or some other factor.

Repeat with as many species as possible.

Project 77

Distribution by Flowering Times

by W. Brett Hornby   [S–I]

Select a number (say six or ten) common, easily recognized flowering
plants. Define an area to be covered—within the normal ambit of the

group. Make outline maps on a large scale—use a scale which will conveniently locate specimens in small areas. Use one map tracing for each
species; plot, using symbols and colours, the location of specimens when
first seen in bloom.

'Late' and 'early' districts may become apparent or a general trend
across country may be seen which may be correlated with altitude, frost
pockets, etc.

Project 78

Celandine and Centipede—A Study in Variation

by F. A. Turk   [S–I]

In the West Country the lesser celandine is an abundant early spring
flower and the large variation to be found in the number of its petals
will serve as a useful introduction, at a simple level, to the phenomena
of variation and their treatment.

Count the petals of each of at least a thousand flowers occurring
over an area as wide as possible in any locality and designed to include
as many habitats as possible. For each clump of flowers so counted,
note the exact habitat, i.e. wall, hedge, open field, marsh, etc., and the
presence or absence of shelter in the vicinity. Graph the results,
entering the number of petals on the vertical axis against the number of
flowers with each given number of petals on the horizontal axis.

What kind of curve do you have on your graph?

Can you demonstrate anything more clearly by summarizing your
results as a histogram?

Can you see any obvious explanation for the results that you have?

Is there any evidence that this variation is under selection by the
environment?

If you have two major peaks to your graph what might you suspect
about the population of celandines in your locality?

In what way does this kind of variation differ from, say, that of the
varying heights of the children in the class?

Collect some of the long, white, intricately knotted centipedes that
live in soils in your locality. (These are Geophilid centepedes sometimes,
quite mistakenly, called 'wire worms'—a name that should be reserved
for the larvae of click beetles.) You should have as many as possible from
as many habitats as possible. Count the number of the pairs of legs on

each of these irrespective of size, colour, etc., of the animal to which they belong. Probably one will have to make do with about a hundred specimens but obviously the more the better.

How do the two graphs (i.e. for centipede and celandine) differ?

Can you suggest anything else you would like to do to test your suggestion?

Project 79

Transplantation

by R. Wilson   [S–I]

The purpose of this project is to discover whether plants of the same species, growing in different areas, are specifically adapted to prevailing conditions. If the project is to succeed, *a large number of species must be transplanted from each area.*

It is necessary for transplanting to be carried out after rain, when the sun is in, so as to avoid wilting, Remove plants of each of the chosen species from, (i) an area of deep shade to open ground, (ii) from open ground to shade. In order to avoid disturbing the plants too much, large amounts of soil should be removed. Polythene bags can be used for transporting plants. Water the plants on transplanting, and for several days after this.

Collect seeds from the plants of the chosen species in the contrasted areas, and germinate them in the laboratory in pots or boxes. They can then be planted in the alternative area. Move other seeds straight from one area to the other.

Warning: Many factors affect presence or absence of particular plants in any one place, not least the presence or absence of parents, and this in itself is worth pursuing. Do not jump to conclusions about single factors unless you are sure you have isolated them from all others [e.g. root competition versus shade under beech trees. In this case, dig with a spade a small plot under a beech tree and remove all roots severed during the digging; seeds or plants should then be placed inside and outside the prepared plot, to test the effect of the competition] .

Project 80

Investigation into the Modes of Support in Hedgerow Climbing Plants

[S–I–A]

(a) Note down the types of plants in an area of hedge, such as on one side of a field.

(b) Note the relative numbers of self-supporting plants, e.g. hazel, hawthorn, blackthorn, and climbing plants, e.g. honeysuckle, wild rose, bramble, convolvulus.

(c) Study the variety of methods adopted by climbing plants in seeking support.

Honeysuckle — a climbing plant

(*d*) For advanced work a comparative study could be made of the stem anatomy of a twining plant such as honeysuckle and a self-supporting plant. Note the poor development of vascular tissue in the climber, and make other comparisons.

Project 81

Influence of Weather Conditions on Growth of Toadstools

by W. P. K. Findlay   [S–I–A]

Mark out in a pasture or piece of woodland a measured area in which past experience has shown a likelihood of a variety of fungal species appearing.

1. From September 1 to November 30 estimate weekly—
   (*a*) the total number of fresh fungal sporophores per unit area, disregarding all old specimens;
   (*b*) the number of different species so far as can be ascertained;
   (*c*) the number of specimens of certain easily recognized dominant species.

2. *Either* record daily rainfall and maximum and minimum temperatures, *or* obtain from the nearest weather station, records of the precipitation and mean temperatures for the period concerned, plus the records for the preceding month.

3. Prepare histograms illustrating total number of fungi collected each week and plot these against the data for rainfall and temperatures. Attempt to find answers to the following questions:
   (*a*) How long after rain do, (i) small species appear?
                                    (ii) large species appear?
   (*b*) Are fungi on stumps and logs affected as quickly by rainfall as are soil inhabiting species?

Project 82

English Names for Lichens

by H. G. Hurrell   [I]

The Observer's Book of Lichens (Published by Warne) gives information and illustrations for the identification of many species. Unfortunately hardly any lichens have English names. It is suggested that pupils identify half a dozen common, conspicuous and distinctive lichens and against the Latin names write their own suggestions for English names. A sketch or photograph of each species would be desirable.

Examples of lichens

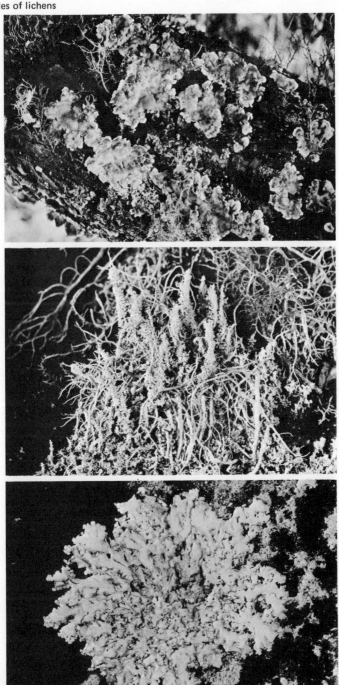

Project 83

Association of Plants and Fungi

by W. P. K. Findlay

Note the principal common toadstools that grow in various typical habitats including the following:

> Woodland of broadleaved trees,
> Woodland of coniferous trees,
> Pastures and lawns,
> Dung heaps and animal droppings,
> Stumps and fallen logs.

This project could be extended to a study of the fungi associated with particular trees, e.g.

Agarics and Boletes associated with trees a mycorrhizal symbionts;
Polypores growing parasitically on trees—noting particularly fungi on unusual hosts as, for instance, the Jews Ear Fungus on a tree other than Elder.

A common tree fungus

Project 84

Productivity in Bluebells

by A. J. Gray   [I–A]

This project on the bluebell, *Endymion non-scriptus*, is directed towards
answering what appear to be simple questions of its ecology: Is it
true that bluebells are more commonly found in shaded environments
than in open ones? If so, do they prefer shade, require shade, tolerate
shade or simply avoid well illuminated habitats?

   Some answers can be provided by measuring the variation in performance in relation to light conditions. A number of bluebell populations
in what appear to be a range of shade conditions should be measured.
Light intensity is best measured by a pair of photocells pointing downward onto a white sheet of paper, one measuring the intensity on the
paper held over the plants, the other on the paper in a nearby completely
open area (clearing, field, top of tree). The operators should be in voice
communication and ensure that they take readings at exactly the same
time. (A pair of photographic exposure meters could be adapted for this
operation.) A uniformly covered sky gives the best conditions.

   Having obtained a set of relative light intensities (and correcting to
allow for variations in the 'full daylight' readings) it is possible to go
ahead and measure performance in the populations of bluebells at
these sites. Two aspects of performance are worth considering—the
average number of capsules per plant and the number of seeds per
capsule. (These are best counted in July.) These results can then be
plotted against light intensity. Any trends which become discernible
should stimulate discussion and can introduce students to the basic
ecological principles of competition, niche selection and reproductive
capacity.

Project 85

The Distribution of Hairy and Glabrous Foxgloves

by A. J. Gray   [A]

If our current thinking about the process of evolution is correct we
must expect that there are good reasons for two or more forms of the

same species being commonly found in nature. Both forms, or variants, must be sufficiently abundant that the rarer could not be maintained in the population by recurrent mutation. An example of such a polymorphism is the existence of hairy and hairless plants of the glove (*Digitalis purpurea*).

In the classic examples of polymorphism (such as industrial melanism in the Peppered Moth (*Biston betulana*) it has been demonstrated that the differential distributions of the two forms (normal v melanic) is related to factors of selection. In the case of the foxglove we have yet to discover whether the relative distribution of the two forms can be detected. What is needed is the sort of basic information which school children can collect, record and discuss. Where do the hairy plants grow? Do the two forms occur together (which they do)? Is the soil different (more acid, wetter, stonier) in places where one form is most commonly found? Are the woods or hedgerows in which the two species are found different in any way (more shaded, disturbed, well vegetated)? Do hairy stems give their possessor any advantage?

The character is best seen in June or July when those plants containing the hairy gene are easily distinguished by the thick 'pelt' of hairs on the stem and the petioles of the rosette leaves. The glabrous plants have thus a distinctly darker looking, redder stem. The mode of inheritance is simple (single gene, hairy dominant)—it may well be worth asking the more advanced scholars whether this is likely to have a long-term effect on the proportions of the two types in any population.

Other, rather more complex, woodland polymorphisms are suitable subjects for such basic distribution studies—pin and thrum primroses, 'hairy' and 'warty' birches, or the variation pattern in spittlebugs (the 'cuckoo spit' insect)—and provide introductions to the concepts of population genetics, speciation and selection.

Project 86

Heath Rush

by G. P. Harris   [A]

It is thought that there is a relationship between altitude, and the morphology and fertility of the inflorescence of *Juncus squarrosus* the Heath Rush.

The abundance of this plant at all altitudes on Dartmoor should provide ample opportunity for tackling this project.

Select plots 2 m x 2 m at, say, 30 m vertical intervals, throughout the range of occurrence of the species. During a single season visit each plot regularly and measure height of inflorescence from ground, diameter at inflorescence and (with calipers) diameter of single flower.

At the appropriate point, compare timing of development of ovum, and by collecting carfully labelled seeds from each plot, and sowing them in pots in the laboratory,.test their fertility. (A climatic record should be kept throughout the exercise.)

Project 87

Heath Rush and *Coleophora*

by D. Welch   [A]

Caterpillars of the moth *Coleophora alticolella* live in the capsules on the inflorescence of *Juncus squarrosus*. The are easily seen because they produce a white case which projects from the capsule about September time.

Since these caterpillars depend on *Juncus* seeds for food, the distribution of the moth is controlled by the performance of the rush (Project 86). It would be interesting to find the altitudinal limit of *Coleophora* in different parts of Dartmoor, and to see if this is related to differences in the seed setting of *Juncus squarrosus*. Furthermore, observations could be made each year to show up changes in the altitudinal limit caused by climatic factors.

Peasall's *Mountains and Moorlands* (New Naturalist) is a good introduction to the subject. Welch (Journal of Animal Ecology, 1965) summaries Studies in the northern Pennines.

Project 88

Effect of Plants on Environment

by G. P. Harris   [A]

Investigate the microclimate in moss tussocks and other masses of vegetation at different times of the day and year. Possible measurements are:

Temperature,   humidity,   pH.

Project 89

Dartmoor Lichens

by G. P. Harris   [A]

To investigate the factors affecting the distribution of certain easily identifiable lichens on Dartmoor.

Method

The following common or distinctive species are suitable for the project:

> *Umbilicaria pustulata*
> *Parmelia omphalodes*
> *Parmelia conspersa*
> *Parmelia furfuracea*
> *Stereocaulon coralloides*
> *Sphaerophorus fragilis*

For one or more of the above species accurately record the following data:

1. Date.
2. Locality (6 or 8 figure map reference).
3. Altitude within 8 m.
4. Aspect, i.e. Whether on vertical, oblique or horizontal surface, and the compass point to which the surface is facing.
5. Whether exposed or sheltered.
6. Condition of plant, i.e. whether stunted or well grown and 'fruiting' abundantly.

A well defined area should be chosen, for example a river valley, group of tors, or a kilometre grid square. Once the species is easily recognized, an individual or small group can produce many records in quite a short time.

The final writing up could be supported by specimens, drawings and photographs.

Project 90

Zonation of Lichens on Tree Trunks

by G. P. Harris   [A]

This zonation has been demonstrated but the factors involved are not known.

To determine zonation the best methods are:

(a) Point quadrats
(b) Short line quadrats
(c) Small square quadrats

Possible factors to be investigated are:

Humidity
Light intensity
Water content of bark
Wind speed
Aspect
Slope
Mineral content of bark

Woodlands especially in Devon, provide excellent conditions for such study.

PONDS AND RIVERS

Project 91

Pond Succession

by W. Brett Hornby   [S]

This idea is based on experience with a simply-made garden pond. A
hole of suitable size (largely dependent on man power) is cleared of sharp
stones and lined with heavy black polythene. When filled with water
this type of pond is initially devoid of life, apart, that is, from bacteria,
windborne spores, etc. If, while the pond is under construction, some
Elodea is placed in 'quarantine' in an aquarium tank indoors, this weed
can be used to furnish the pond without too great a chance of introducing creatures.

Most interesting records can now be gathered of the kind and
numbers of living things which colonize this virgin territory. It is very
surprising how soon a thriving, mixed population grows from small insect
larvae to frogs and newts. If, later, fish are introduced, a new set of
observations can be made of the changes (e.g. a numerous colony of
Notonecta subsequently disappeared).

The construction of a pond itself is a most valuable contribution to
the welfare of wild life at a time when older ponds are being filled in or
are being made useless by neglect.

Project 92

Recording the Development of Toad Tadpoles

by K. Watkins   [S–I]

Toads spawn during March and April and their eggs can be easily found
as strings of small black dots encased in ribbons of jelly-like substance
deposited in ponds and slow moving waterways.

When the eggs hatch the tadpoles should be studied closely and drawn or photographed at weekly intervals.

The drawings or photographs will show the development of the tadpole from its earliest form immediately after hatching from the egg to its final change into a very small toad. This whole process takes between nine and fifteen weeks, according to weather conditions.

Each illustration should be accompanied with the date it was made, the temperature of the water and air, and the weather conditions prevailing during the previous week.

Malcolm Smith, in his book, *The British Amphibians and Reptiles* (New Naturalist Series No. 20), observes that the temperature of the external air, which may in turn control the growth of the Algae on which the tadpoles largely feed, *appears* to be the most important factor in the time the tadpoles take to develop.

Work on this subject, providing it is backed up by careful and accurate water and air temperature readings, could be of value.

The project could equally well be applied to frogs and newts.

Project 93

Ponds

by John Clegg   [S–I–A]

Both village and farm ponds are disappearing rapidly and yet they are invaluable for biology teaching. Information is required regarding as many ponds in Devon as possible. There are not very many in the County, although there may be one in the vicinity of your school.

If so, note its situation, size and, particularly, the common plants and animals which live in and around it. Do not worry about ones you find too hard to identify. Visit the pond regularly throughout the year, noting the date of each visit and the plants and animal species observed each time.

Please send a preliminary note to the address below as to the situation of the pond, then forward your lists of plant and animal species at the end of the year.

John Clegg, c/o Devon Trust for Nature Conservation, 2 Pennydaraina Road, Exeter, EX4 6BQ.

Project 94

How do Frogs find their Way to their Breeding Ponds?

by K. Watkins [A]

Malcolm Smith, in his book *The British Amphibians and Reptiles* (New Naturalist Series No. 20), asks the above question. He continues: 'We do not know the answer. We know that the animals return to the same ponds year after year—but are they the same frogs that go back? And what guides those frogs that, having become sexually mature, seek a pond for the first time? Frog spawn in a greater variety of ponds than toads. The district in which Savage made his observations was some 2200 m long by 800 m broad as measured on the map, but was crossed by two ridges of hills each about 10 m high. It contained fifteen ponds and it must have been difficult for a frog living in that area to travel far in any direction without meeting water of some sort. Yet only certain ponds were chosen. Savage believes that there is enough evidence to show that it is the smell of the pond—the essential oils produced by the plants—which directs the frogs. The theories of Hydrotaxis, Geotaxis and voice as guiding factors, which have been put forward, are dismissed by him as untenable. Warm, wet nights certainly favour migration, but movements may take place on nights where there is **no** rain at all. The direction of the wind from the water to the frogs is of importance.'

It is suggested that the sixth form biologist should investigate practically, and in the literature, ways of testing frogs' navigational ability.

Project 95

National Mapping Scheme for Land and Freshwater Molluscs

by S. M. Turk [I—A]

This scheme lends itself readily to long or short term projects, whilst adding to the knowledge of mollusc distribution on a national basis.

The method of recording is simple. The Conchological Society of Great Britain and Ireland, under whose aegis the Census is operated,

issue record cards on which the name of every British species of non-
marine mollusc appears in abbreviated form. The names are crossed
through as they are discovered. Local comparative mollusc ecology
can be conveniently studied by school groups on this basis of recording.
Finds of exceptional interest to the Recorder may be written up on
special individual record cards.

A secondary but important aspect of the scheme is to ascertain which
species are found only near houses and cultivated land, evidence that
they have probably been distributed by man. Devon is one of the
counties of particular interest in this respect since several species found
only in association with humans elsewhere in Britain, occur 'wild' in
the south-west of the country.

Ease and accuracy in identification can soon be achieved with careful practice, especially if a school type-collection is started: in so far as
specific identification is the basis of all detailed ecological work, such a
collection will prove its value over the years. The excellent book by
Horst Janus *The young specialist looks at Molluscs*, published by Burke
and Co. in 1965, is recommended for identification and as a basic guide
to known distribution. More detailed distribution notes and maps on
the vice-county system are to be found in A Census of the distribution
of British non-marine Mollusca by A. E. Ellis (*Journal of Conchology*
(1951) vol. 23, Nos. 6 & 7, obtainable from the Secretary of the Conchological Society, T. E. Crowley, B.Sc., The Cottage, Church Road,
Bampton, Oxon., together with the 1966 supplement).

The basic object of the Census is to obtain as complete a list as
possible of the species living at the present (i.e. since 1950) in each of
the 10 kilometre squares of the British National Grid. Eventually an
Atlas on the lines of the Botanical Society *Atlas of the British Flora*
will be produced. Cards, notes for the guidance of records and help
with the identification of difficult species may be obtained from the
Recorder for non-marine Molluscs, Dr. M. P. Kerney, Dept. of Geology,
Imperial College, Prince Consort Road, London, S.W.7.

Ramshorn pond snail (*Planorbis corneus*) — a freshwater mollusc

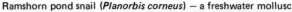
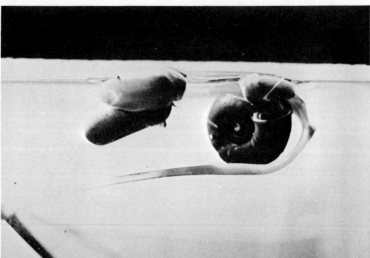

Project 96

Pond Life

by Alan W. Heath   [I–A]

The main questions asked in this work are WHAT lives WHERE, WHEN, and WHY? Random dips in a pond seldom do more than provide some specimens for study, and it is desirable to set out a programme of work to do. The writer has successfully used the following system for many years with considerable satisfaction.

(a) Select a suitable pond to study. Obtain permission to get samples if it is on private land, and select one which is preferably undisturbed, i.e. by fishermen. The pond may be large or small, but collect from the same site each time. Other sites may be included if time permits.

(b) Write up a description of the pond, its grid reference and height above sea level, and draw a rough map on a scale sufficient to show nearby trees, vegetation, etc.

(c) Try to identify all the local vegetation both in the water and near to it.

(d) Always use the same *plankton net* and ascertain the number of mesh per square inch.

(e) Take the same number of sweeps in a regular interval of time, e.g. 7 sweeps in 6 minutes at each visit, remembering not to sweep too quickly.

(f) Record *air temperature* at the site and also *water temperature* (before you disturb the water with the net). Record also the pH. A pH Comparator is ideal here, but pH test papers will suffice.

(g) Note the *previous weather* and also the *present weather*, especially if there has been recent heavy rain. Note if the water has *ice* on it, and if so what thickness this is.

(h) Note the condition of the water. Is it still or are there ripples caused by the wind? Is it clear or cloudy? Note the extent of the vegetation on the bottom and at the sides as well as in the water.

(i) Examine the collected sample as soon as possible, at least within a couple of days.

Recording

The following simple method of counting has proved successful:

1. If only one specimen is seen they are considered to be VERY RARE.
2. If two or three are seen they are considered to be RARE.

3. When up to ten are seen they are considered to be OCCASIONAL.
4. Between 10 and 20 they are considered to be COMMON.
5. Fairly plentiful they are considered to be FREQUENT.
6. Obviously plentiful they are considered to be ABUNDANT.
7. Very many seen they are considered to be VERY ABUNDANT.
8. Sample is absolutely crowded with the specimen DOMINANT.
   DOMINANT REGIONS are sometimes used to show local colonies and regions where algae are localized in great quantity.

It is a good idea to record the specimens as a histogram on graph paper with the specimen listed on the vertical side and the date on the horizontal. Make it large enough to cover a year, and the date can be at about fortnightly intervals as this is usually frequent enough. Fill in the number of squares to correspond to the number on the table given, i.e. one square means very rare, four squares means common, and so on. Air, water temperature, and pH can be recorded on a normal graph.

Project 97

Frogs and Toads

by Maxwell Knight   [I–A]

A possible task in connection with *the local populations of frogs and toads.*

For some years now, naturalists have noticed a very marked decrease in the numbers of common frogs in many areas, and to some degree a falling off in toad populations as well. There are probably several reasons for this:

1. Over-collecting by professional frog-catchers in the case of frogs.
2. The disappearance of breeding ponds due to neglect, filling in for building operations, etc.
3. In some districts, where toxic sprays have been used on land near to breeding ponds, the small insects on which the 'baby' frogs and toads rely when they leave the water, may possibly have become so reduced as to affect the numbers of survivors.
4. Road traffic could also be a factor, as many *toads* get run over at night when migrating to their spawning places in early spring.

Whether all or some of these factors are the answer, it would be an interesting exercise to make a survey of those ponds known in the past to be used by these amphibians for breeding.

The object would be to find out how many of such ponds are still used and to endeavour to ascertain why those still reasonably 'healthy'

A common toad (*Bufo bufo*) and (*right*) the distinctive strings of toad's spawn

may now be avoided by amphibians, and how many have disappeared altogether.

Preliminary work could be done in the autumn and winter months by mapping the ponds.

In the western counties frogs spawn earlier than the colonies further east, and observations on usable ponds could well be started in late January if the weather is not severe. Toads can be expected by mid-February onwards.

The information to be sought should come under the following headings:

(a) Does the pond in question have breeding colonies of frogs, toads, or possibly both?
(b) Date of arrival and prevailing weather at that time.
(c) Routes taken (in the case of toads).
(d) Numbers of casualties.
(e) Estimated numbers of males and females.
(f) Dates of spawn, hatching and progress of tadpoles.
(g) Dates of leaving the water.
(h) Any subsequent observations on the presence of froglets and toadlets; and also of adults seen in various places—gardens, fields, ditches and so on.

There are, of course, many other points that could be included for more senior pupils, but the suggested records have been kept reasonably simple so as to attract Juniors to the work without scaring them off with with too many questions.

Project 98

Stickleback Salinity Experiment

by Colin A. Howes   [A]

The three-spined stickleback *Gasterosterus aculeatus* is a common fish
in ponds, streams and rivers throughout the west country. Students
wishing to undertake this project should familiarize themselves with
the identity of this species in order that specimens can be collected for
experimentation.

The three-spined stickleback is found in waters of very diverse levels
of salinity, from freshwater streams to the brackish waters of river
estuaries; it has even been recorded in rock pools around our coastline.
Although this species is not a true marine fish, its close relative the
fifteen-spined stickleback *Spinachia vulgaris* is only to be found in the
sea.

For an organism to move from fresh water to salt water and back to
freshwater—as seen to be the case in the three-spined stickleback—
requires a great deal of tolerance of differing osmotic pressures.

As osmosis forms the basis of the experiments, it would be advisable
for teachers in charge of the project to brief pupils in the elements of
osmosis and diffusion with special reference to freshwater and marine
teliosts (bony fish).

Aims

1. To determine what percentage of seawater the three-spined stickleback is able to tolerate.
2. (*a*) To discover how quickly the stickleback is able to reach this
   optimum level of tolerance, and
   (*b*) How quickly it can revert back to life in a freshwater
   environment.

Experiments (*a*) and (*b*) of 2 are designed to ascertain the time taken
by the stickleback to adjust its physiological processes to accommodate
for seawater mingling with fresh in an estuary at high tide, then the
reversal of osmotic conditions when the tide goes out again, confirming
the results with the normal time taken for the tide to ebb and flow.

Method

For the experiments at least ten specimens should be used, preferably
more. Collect the sticklebacks from similar habitats, thus ensuring that
their osmotic tolerance is approximately uniform. Keep them in

separate containers in order to obtain accurate results from each
individual and also to avoid rivalry.

To find the optimum per cent of seawater tolerable, move the specimens up only a few per cent at a time, giving at least a complete day at
each level. It is obvious that for each set of experiments a new batch of
specimens will be required. Experiments 2 will be the reverse of 1, i.e.
the first stage will be the longest period of time for the change, decreasing the time spent at each level until the shortest average time for
reversion is discovered.

Notes

If it is impossible to obtain seawater, it is possible to make it artificially
in two ways:

	Grammes per litre
1. Sodium chloride	23.476
Magnesium chloride	4.981
Sodium sulphate	3.917
Calcium chloride	1.102
Potassium chloride	0.664
Sodium bicarbonate	0.096
Boracic acid	0.026
Strontium chloride	0.024
Sodium fluoride	0.003
2. Sodium chloride	45½ oz
Potassium chloride	1¼ oz
Calcium chloride (anhydrous)	2 oz
Magnesium chloride	8¾ oz
Magnesium sulphate	11½ oz
Sodium bicarbonate	1/5 oz
Mix with 10 gallons of water and add	
Potassium nitrate	1/5 oz
Sodium sulphate	10 grains
Iron chloride	5 grains

Natural seawater tends to go off if kept for a long period of time; this
can be averted by regular filtering through an old stocking.

Project 99

Freshwater Limpets in Devon

by G. P. Harris   [A]

The aim here is to investigate the distribution of the freshwater limpet in Devonshire rivers.

Within a particular reach of a river it should be possible to establish relationships between the distribution of the limpet and water speed and oxygen content. These animals are well distributed in most Devon rivers and should provide plenty of good material for study.

A similar project could be attempted using Planarians.

SEASHORE

Project 100

Use of the Drift Line

by R. Wilson   [S]

One of the most interesting areas along the shore is, undoubtedly, the
drift line. Simple lists made of the objects which are found stranded
along this line can often lead to interesting biological discoveries.

Firstly, make a simple list of *all* the different objects found along
the drift line. This should be done after a low tide, when the sea is
relatively calm, and after heavy seas, when there has been a high tide. If
each member of a group studies a part of the drift line, then a large area
can be covered.

A complete list should be compiled from the group lists, and the
possible source of origin of the objects indicated.

Some of the entries can be looked at in detail, and various problems
posed. How have certain animals become stranded? What affect does the
current have on the animals? Are more animals washed up after a spring
tide, than after a neap tide? What special adaptation do (*a*) seaweeds
have (*b*) seashore animals, so that they can normally resist these forces?
How do these sea-shore creatures feed? Movement of species can be
investigated, reproduction (necessity for fish to lay large numbers of
eggs); effects of high tide on the coastline; erosion and accretion; the
dependence of animals on the sea for food, etc.

Project 101

Seashell Studies

by S. M. Turk   [S—I—A]

The study of strand lines by making quadrat counts at regular or
irregular intervals, always correlating these with time of year and condition of weather and tide, will give interesting results. A useful extension
of the study would be to establish which strand shells actually occur
alive in the immediate vicinity: the effects of long shore drift vary from

place to place, sometimes even sorting left valves from right. Schools in different parts of the country could carry out linked projects on the above lines, comparing strand-line and live species in the separated areas. Many molluscs are confined to the south-west, being replaced by quite different species in north-east Britain. Moreover, species found living between tide-marks in comparatively frost-free districts may occur only off-shore elsewhere.

Project 102

Winkle Zonation

by Colin A. Howes   [I]

Here is a simple experiment designed to investigate the zonation of peri-winkles on rocky shorelines. The experiment also illustrates the influence of horizontal zonation on marine plant and animal life.

Theory

The basic inter-tidal zones are as follows:

> Splash zone
> Upper shore
> Middle shore
> Lower shore
> Sub-littoral fringe

which are observed as successive horizontal belts of different species of seaweed between high and low water levels.

It is important that you learn to distinguish between the four commonly found species of winkle—

> *Littorina neritoides*—least periwinkle
> *Littorina saxatilis*—rough periwinkle
> *Littorina littoralis* (obtusata)—flat periwinkle
> *Littorina littorea*—Common or edible periwinkle

Correctly identified specimens can be borrowed from many Natural History Museums.

Experiments

1. *Aim*—To determine the dominant species of winkle in each zone at low tide. Method—Work in groups, one on each zone, and by the use of quadrats work out the percentage populations in each zone.

2. The Dominant Species for each zone having been established, the second experiment can commence.

   Aim—To see how far winkles move within their zone and to what extent they move into adjoining zones.

   Method—An equal number of dominant winkles from each zone is marked with a serial number and released in situ, frequent visits being made to discover how far and in which direction they have moved.

   Marking—The serial number can be applied in Indian Ink, sealed over when dry by a clean varnish. The number must be entered into a log book, together with information about species, zone, point of release, columns being left for data on length and direction of movement which will be gathered on subsequent visits.

LOG BOOK			
SPECIES	SERIAL NUMBER	ZONE	RECAPTURE NOTES

3. *Aim*—To investigate the homing abilities of winkles by removing a number of zone dominant species to other zones, to see if they are capable of returning to their normal zone, and if so how long it takes.

   Method—Collect three groups of winkles, each group containing equal numbers of zone dominant species. Each individual must be numbered, its species and point of release being entered in the log book.

   Each group is then released, one in each of the major zones. At daily or weekly intervals, checks should be made on the progress of each individual, noting distance and direction travelled from the point of release, the results being entered on a large scale chart of the area.

Project 103

Movement of Sand along the Beach (or in a Dune System)

by A. P. Carr   [I]

A partially-stabilized sand-dune

Join end-to-end two or three sticky fly papers of the old type. These should be supported by a strip of hardboard of similar width, and this is erected vertically on a stake. Probably the best way of joining the fly papers to the hardboard is by means of a stapler. Examine how high up the sand moves on windy days. If it is possible, use a hand anemometer to find the wind strength at the time and see if there is any obvious relationship of height, quantity and wind strength (is the sand wet or dry?).

It may even be possible to weigh the different fly papers before and after the experiment, to see the relative amount deposited, providing care is taken to remove the papers and a suitable balance is available to make the measurements.

This experiment gives an idea of relative rates, but the method does produce turbulence so that the answers one gets are not quite those which you would obtain by other methods.

Project 104

Investigation into Heights and Root Depths of Coastal Species

by R. Wilson   [I—A]

This project can be tackled in one of two ways: either as an investigation of a number of species in one particular habitat, or it can be an investigation of species which occur in various habitats.

(a) Investigation of species in one habitat.
     It appears that prevailing conditions affect the root and shoot length of plants on the sand-dunes. To carry out this investigation, a large number of species is required.
     Choose a number of species which occur on sand-dunes. Three zones should be selected: suggested zones—leeside of dunes nearest sea; seaside of dunes nearest sea; crest of dunes.
     A small number of plants of the same species are carefully removed, and the roots and aerial parts measured accurately. These can be plotted on a graph and comparison made.
     Alternatively, if there are a number of dunes, of differing ages, then one zone for a number of dunes, e.g. the seaside of three dunes, can be selected. The same procedure should be carried out.

(b) A number of species which are found in various habitats, within the coastal region, should be selected. Plants which grow on the sand and those which grow on the shingle can be compared. Root and shoot measurements should be taken, and comparisons made.

Remember that sand dunes (and shingle beaches) are very sensitive habitats—easily damaged by trampling and sliding. In this and all exercises on dunes great care should be taken to disturb the surface as little as possible.

Project 105

Investigation of Dune Soils

by R. Wilson   [I–A]

If there are sand dunes in the vicinity of your school, with a succession of very young to very old dunes, it is possible to make a survey of the dune soils.

Each dune should be investigated in the following regions:

(*a*) seaside,   (*b*) crest,   (*c*) leeside,

and three vertical zones should be examined in each region at the following depths below the surface:

(i) 10 cm,   (ii) 20 cm,   (iii) 30 cm.

The following are suggestions for factors to be investigated:

1. pH value   2. humus content
3. water holding capacity   4. water content
5. permeability   6. soil profile.

If plant cover is also taken into account, it will be possible to correlate plant species with the various soil factors.

Project 106

Zonation Work on the Seashore

by M. C. F. Proctor   [I–A]

Many questions may be answered by careful observation or repeated visits to a rocky shore.

Which species grow only below the low water mark of neap tides and are hence exposed only in spring?

Which species can grow above high water mark of neaps and can thus withstand regular exposure for more than twelve hours at a stretch?

Do the species of rock pools bear any relation to those of open rock surfaces in the vicinity, or lower down the shore?

Which species are confined to pools?

Do the seaweed flora differ on rock faces of different slope, aspect, or exposure?

How is the high water mark of springs related to the upper limit of inter-tidal organisms, and to the lower limit of land plants?

Where do distribution limits lie in relation to lines of regular submergence by spring tides, wave-wash or occasional submergence, spray?

The maritime flowering plants and lichens should not be forgotten; their distributions are as interesting as those of the seaweeds.

References

BALLANTYNE, W. J., 'A biologically-defined exposure scale for the comparative description of rocky shores', *Field studies,* 1961, **1** (3), 1–19.
MOYSE, J. and NELSON-SMITH, A., 'Zonation of Animals and Plants on Rocky Shores around Dale, Pembrokeshire', *Field Studies,* 1963, **1** (5), 1–31.

Project 107

Survey Work on the Seashore

by M. C. F. Proctor   [I–A]

Observations on shore zonation provide a great deal of scope for simple levelling and surveying. Transects may be levelled up the shore, so that zonation can be related to tidal levels, etc.

It is particularly interesting to compare shores of differing degrees of exposure in this way.

A shore can be roughly contoured by placing a series of stakes at the water's edge at predetermined intervals as the tide falls. Photographs are an excellent way of recording the main features of zonation on a shore, the character of the seaweed cover at representative points, and seasonal variations.

An example of a zonation chart is shown on page 173.

ZONATION OF A FEW COMMON SEAWEEDS AND ANIMALS ON
A ROCKY SHORE

Project 108

National Survey of Marine Molluscs

by S. M. Turk [I–A]

There is much to be learnt about the ecology, life-histories and geographical distribution of marine molluscs. The object of the survey is primarily distributional, but, whenever possible, data on habitats and behaviour is being collected and filed. In 1961 the coastal waters of the British Isles were divided into forty clearly defined Census Areas by a sub-committee of the Conchological Society of Great Britain and Ireland for recording purposes.

The aim is to record as many as possible of the species present in each and every Area, thereby revealing over-all national patterns of distribution for common as well as rare species. Special categories are recognized for species found in the living state (*a*), empty shells (*b*), and empty worn shells (*c*). It is surprising how few reputable collectors of the past specified whether their records were based on living animals or empty shells. A prototype recording form has been designed so that recorders can fill in the desirable information under appropriate headings. As soon as sufficient numbers of reliable records have accumulated, a provisional census will be produced.

A group studying the shell life of a particular area or one or two beaches within the Area, can help not only the Conchological Society's work, but may be helped in turn with identification checks by the Marine Recorder. The formation of a type collection will facilitate identification.

Recognizing the difficulties involved in all specialist study these days, the Conchological Society issues a series of 'Papers for Students' on various aspects of Conchology. For details, write to the Officer in Charge of Juniors, Rev. J. E. J. Biggs, 48 Park Road, Bromley, Kent.

The main project of identifying together with recording observations on ecology and behaviour offers in itself a useful discipline in school work, but many sidelines may suggest themselves.

Project 109

Limpets, Winkles, and Crevices

by S. M. Turk   [A]

1. Interesting studies can be made on the three species of British limpets (*Patella*) in relation to their ecological and geographical distribution. As *Patella depressa* is a south-western species, the Devonshire coast is one of the few counties where all three species live. Studies on the remaining two species may still be undertaken on other parts of the coast, except between the Isle of Wight and Humber where only *Patella vulgata* has been recorded. On this part of the coast observations on the variation of the living animal (easily replaced on the rocks after examination) should reveal a remarkable range of variants,

Limpets — one of the most common univalves found on our shores

superficially resembling one or other of the absent species. *Homing* of limpets is another possible project, conducted by plotting the positions of specimens in a small area, marking them and recording subsequent positions in relation to time, tide and weather.

2. Research on the distribution and density patterns of the least winkle, *Littorina neritoides*, above high-water mark, will reveal a marked relation to the splash and spray to which the position is exposed. This is one of the species used as a biological exposure 'meter'.

3. Investigation into the crevice mollusc fauna of a particular beach. Not only rock cracks and crevices but empty barnacle shells may afford shelter for several different species of small size. For further details of the Marine Census Survey work write to Mrs. S. M. Turk, Marine Recorder, 'Shang-ri-La', Reskadinnick, Camborne, Cornwall.

References

BARRET, J., and YONGE, C. M. *Pocket Guide to the Sea Shore* (London, Collins).
FRETTER, Dr. V. and GRAHAM, Prof. A., *British Pros. branch Molluscs* (London, Ray Society, 1962).
TEBBLE, N., *British Bivalve Seashells* (London, British Museum (Natural History).
TURK. S. M., *Collecting Shells* (London, Foyles).

Project 110

The Diurnal Activity of the Invertebrate Fauna of a Sand Dune

by F. A. Turk   [A]

Sand dunes provide a most useful and easily defined habitat for element-ary animal ecological investigation: the number of species is relatively small and so the problem of identification is at a minimum whilst the physical characteristics of the environment are rather easily isolated and their interaction simpler than in most other habitats.

It will probably be found best to limit the project, in the first instance, to arthropods, (insects, spiders, harvestmen, mites, woodlice being almost the only groups involved in this instance) and the number of species of each is not large. It should be noted however, at the commencement of the work, that the presence of ants, hares, rabbits, cattle or ponies may complicate the findings greatly, so that if time is limited it will then be best to confine the area examined to the unfixed or only partially reclaimed dune.

At different times of the day and in different weather conditions different species seem to dominate the dune whilst the active nocturnal fauna is often quite different from the diurnal one.

At the beginning of the work it is best to spend a little time collecting a specimen or so of each insect and arachnid species encountered and in taking some trouble to identify them. This should be repeated through the season at intervals of about a month as new forms become apparent. The small reference collection so formed and carried in the field will save many hours of work and will simplify the recording.

Make a rough map of the dune indicating the area which you wish to work and the nature of any plant cover. Endeavour to visit the dune at different times of the day and keep a record, in columns, of the following data: date and time of visit; air temperature at 50 cm, 25 cm, 12 cm, 6 cm and 3 cm above the surface of the sand: the temperature of the surface of the sand; the temperature 3 cm, 6 cm, 12 cm, 25 cm below the surface of the sand; the name of the insect or other arthropod found to be active; description of the activity observed, e.g. Pompilid flying, Pompilid crawling on sand, etc. Make this record as complete as possible on as many days as possible. It will be worthwhile when the occasion occurs, to make small excavations around plants and elsewhere and to note any under surface activity. Visits to the dune at, or just before daybreak in midsummer will yield a great deal of data. The records when sufficient should enable you to answer questions like the following:

At what critical temperature does surface activity cease?
Do animals behave on cloudy days in the same way as on sunny ones?
What is the daily rhythm of events in Arthropod activity on the dune?
Do you notice any consistent difference between the activity of carnivorous forms and the species of herbivores and scavengers?
What is the flight activity above the dune?
How does rain effect the activity on and above the dune?

Remember how easy it is to damage a dune.

SOIL

Project 111
Soil Survey

by A. V. Shepley   [I–A]

Aim

To provide a soil map to use either for the study of the soil itself, e.g.
in a rural studies course, or for comparison with surveys of organisms,
particularly both natural and cultivated vegetation.

Method
Equipment

A spade (small size), a knife or scissors, a hand lens, pencil, paper,
polythene bags, and for extensive work only, a soil auger.

Preparation of a soil profile

This is the basic unit of the survey and is the sequence of soil variations
from the surface down to the unaltered material below from which the
soil has developed—the soil parent material. A soil profile is best looked
at as exposed in the side of a freshly dug pit, though fresh exposures
can be made in ditches or road-side cuttings.

1. Cut through any ground vegetation carefully with the spade and
   remove the turves, placing them upside-down on one side to be
   replaced and gently stamped down after the pit has been inspected
   and refilled.

2. Dig the pit until no further changes in colour or texture of the soil
   are observable. Over much of Britain this will be at bed-rock, but
   on sites where the soil is formed from drift, or on rock which is not
   contributing to the soil for other reasons, it may be convenient to
   stop sooner. Plan the pit so that the face to be recorded faces the sun.

3. Prepare the face of the profile as smoothly as possible and remove
   large projecting roots with knife or scissors.

4. Recording of profile details:
   (a) In a field notebook record depth and distribution of colour
       changes, root depth, and changes in texture (see ref.1), starting at
       the top of the profile, i.e. at the turves first removed and
       working downwards. There is an opportunity here for pupils to
       devise their own divisions for texture.

(b) If samples are to be analyzed in the laboratory later they should be taken from the base of the profile upwards, thus avoiding soil from above becoming mixed with later samples. Samples may either be taken at specified depths or where colour changes occur. Samples should be placed in labelled polythene bags (1000 gauge bags are strong enough to be washed and re-used).

(c) Samples of stones may be worth taking, particularly in glacial drift areas. Using the hand lens, they may be checked for the presence of erratics.

(d) A permanent record of the profile is best made photographically. If this is to be done then:

   (i) All roots sticking out of the profile face must be carefully trimmed flush or they will appear of disproportionate size in the photograph.

   (ii) Any crumbs of soil which have been distributed from one layer to another must be carefully brushed away.

   (iii) Profiles must all be in the same moisture state when photo-graphed. (The easiest way to ensure this is to spray them immediately beforehand with a nasal atomizer.)

   (iv) The orientation and quality of the light must be the same.

   (v) A scale should be included.

   (vi) The same brand of film should always be used.

Siting profiles

On a slope it is least confusing to look at the side of the profile lying parallel with the slope.

The actual location of profiles will depend mainly upon the detail with which the soils are to be mapped. Within any one climatic region the soils developed are mainly affected by the parent material, the slope, the drainage and the vegetation. The most economic approach to the preparation of a map is to site key profiles where changes might be expected (an interesting exercise in ecological understanding for older pupils), and then to fill in the boundaries from auger cores, adding extra profiles whenever a previously undetected change occurs.

The map

In most areas significant changes in soil characteristics will occur at intervals frequent enough for maps on the 2½ in. scale, or larger to be prepared. Correlation with Soil Survey maps (see ref. 2) or Geological Survey maps, both drift and solid, may then be made.

Analyses

Laboratory analysis of soil samples is simply carried out for humus content, particle size, and pH—though the value of the latter is frequently over-emphasized in school courses. Most chemical analyses require more sophisticated equipment than is normally available to schools and raise difficulties in the interpretation of results.

Reference

Bulletins and Memoirs of the Soil Survey of England and Wales
(Rothampsted Experimental Station, Harpenden, Herts.)
Field Handbook (Soil Survey of England and Wales, under revision).

Project 112

The Activity of Soil Micro-organisms

by A. V. Shepley   [A]

Aims

Most biology texts refer to the effects of liming, the use of fertilizers, or the effects of humus content of soils on the activity of soil micro-organisms. This investigation enables a relative ranking of samples of different soils or treatments to be arrived at. Considerable refinement of technique would be required to obtain absolute values.

Method

Soil micro-organisms are supplied with optimum growth conditions and the carbon dioxide evolution measured.

1. Wet some air-dried soil, previously passed through a 2 mm sieve, to field capacity by placing in a Buchmer funnel, covering with water, and applying suction from a water pump for a quarter of an hour.

2. Take 100 g of the soil and thoroughly mix with 0.5 g glucose.

3. Place the mixture in a wide-mouthed 250 cm^3 conical flask and gently lower on to its surface a 7.5 cm x 2.5 cm specimen tube containing a known volume (say 10 to 15 cm^3) of N/10 sodium hydroxide solution (4 g sodium hydroxide per litre).

4. Seal the flask with a rubber bung and incubate in an oven or over a radiator at 28–32 $^\circ$C for 24 hours.

5. Remove the specimen tube from the flask and titrate the remaining hydroxide with N/10 hydrochloric acid (3.65 cm^3 conc HCl per litre) using phenolphthalein as an indicator. Before titration

1.0 cm³ 50 per cent barium chloride solution should be added to precipitate the carbonate. Titration should be slow with careful stirring to the pink to colourless end-point.

6. mg CO_2 produced/100 g soil/24 hours
   = (original volume N/10 NaOH − cm³ N/10 HC1 used) x 2.2.

Remarks

This method requires no special apparatus except one burette for the titration. Samples of soil at field capacity can be obtained by taking them from the field about 24 hours after rain which has completely wetted the soil, and provided gas-tight seals can be obtained, almost any containers of about 250 cm³ and 10–20 cm³ capacity can be used. The chemicals involved put classes at minimal risk and illustrate the relevance of chemistry to biology studies.

Project 113

The Reconstruction of a 'Sub-fossil' Landscape

by F. A. Turk   [A]

This project is suitable for groups of, say, five senior students working over four to six months; most of the work can be done during the winter.

In the far south-west of Britain, and elsewhere along the western seaboard, are to be found a series of submarine peat deposits. All lie near the surface although at times under a considerable deposit of sand; they are especially common at the seaward end of drowned river-valleys (rias), e.g. Mounts Bay, Senne, Portmellon, Maenporth, etc. These 'low-level' peats are, generally speaking, of Neolithic age. They contrast with the 'high-level' peats found, for example, buried under clays, sands and superficial peats on parts of Dartmoor and Bodmin Moor. These latter represent interglacial and early post-glacial deposits of the Pleistocene and early Holocene. Of the two, the low level peats seem to be easier to work if only because they are more productive of fairly identifiable fragments of plants and animals, but this by no means precludes work on the others since very few have been examined in detail.

Procure examples of peat, about 0.03 m³ each, from equally spaced stations both up, down and across such a valley or seashore and at suit-ably spaced depths from each. The latter is especially important since, if the animal and plant remains are well preserved and time allows, it would obviously be possible to make a study of the changes in the landscape before its final inundation. Place each sample in a plastic bag, fully label it and store until required. Also make a plan of the site from which each sample was taken and show all the sampling stations on it, the numbers or letters given to each being made to correspond to those on the labels in the plastic bags. The peat can be dug out with spades but better results can be obtained by using one of the earth-borers used by the U.S. army for making latrines in tropical countries and obtainable for a few shillings from some Army Surplus stores.

Pull the peat apart and in a preliminary examination take out the larger fragments of wood, plant roots and stems. Wash the remainder, after further breaking up, through sieves of decreasing mesh. Extract from the residues all insect fragments, seeds and fruits. From the untreated peat left from each sample make a preparation of the pollen grains by any of the simpler methods. In this connection an extremely useful book will be found to be Wodehouse, R. P. (1959) (see References). It is available through the regional libraries scheme.

Seeds should be kept, carefully labelled in small plastic boxes or tubes; pollen grains can be stored as microscopic slide preparations. Insect fragments, with the exception of wings which are best mounted in balsam on glass slides, are stuck with a white paste (photographer's white mountant or a clear paste, e.g. 'Gloy', are best) on to strips of white card. These can be pinned, like carded insect mounts, into a box. The larger pieces of wood will need to be cut transversely and sandpapered on the cut surfaces. Any of the books on wood identification to be found at most country libraries will help to identify these.

Seeds and fruits can be identified by reference to Ross-Craig, S. (1948–1967) (still, alas, unfinished). Much more expeditiously, however, one can use Katz, N. J., Katz, S. V. and Kipiani, M. G. (1965). This book is entirely in Russian but for the present purpose could be used extremely well by anyone knowing not one single word of that language.

Beetle elytra and other parts of these insects can be roughly identified by using Linssen, E. F. (1959). However it will be easier to accomplish more exact identification by comparing the mounted fragments that have been collected, with a collection of British beetles such as is to be found in most county museums.

Reference literature, such as that cited above, and a flora of the British Isles will give the kind of habitat in which each species of plant and animal lives. These should be tabulated in a notebook and those records agreeing in general type should have some distinctive identifying mark added to them. From this list of habitats and species it is possible to reconstruct the whole landscape as it was—often in remarkable detail. Sometimes from one species we may deduce the presence of another, e.g. some beetles are found in certain mosses or on grassy banks, and so with fair probability we may infer such to have been present additionally once we have the record of the beetle. Likewise one record may support another; grains of wild einkorn, emmer and perennial rye were found in these low level peats together with the pollen of the cornflower—a common weed of neolithic fields. From these we may conclude the presence of Man in the vicinity and of his agricultural activity. As a guide to what may be accomplished the following were among the remains identified by the three sixth-formers mentioned above:

> *Seeds and Fruits*—Perennial Rye, Einkorn, Hazel nut, Acorn, Rubus (bramble type), Bogbean seeds, Arrowhead seed.
> *Wood Fragments*—Alder, Hazel, Oak, Elm (Alder commonest at all levels except lower, hence the site is probably getting wetter).
> *Pollen Grains*—Alder (common), Birch, Pine, Hazel, (c), Elm (c), Oak (c), Lime and Yew(?), Cornflower, Jacob's Ladder, Willow-herb, a Composite, Marsh Valerian, Mallow, Goosefoot.
> *Spores*—Common Polypody, Bracken, Royal Fern.
> *Beetles*—*Cymindis Adillaris, Corymbites cupreus* var. *aeruginosus, Tachys pumila, Strophosomus faber, Phyllotreta* sp. (most likely a species feeding on Cruciferae and hence arguing the presence of one of these plants locally, *Phytonomus austriaeus* (proving presence of Trefoils and/or clovers). A weevil larva.
> *Micro-Lepidoptera Eriocephala aruncella* (wing fragment).

As a preliminary exercise a class may like to sketch an hypothetical landscape situated where a valley, in low hills, opens out onto a coastal plain, all aspects included to be based on the items listed above. Group criticism of each drawing will soon show the principles of reconstruction which will have to be employed.

Some of the entries can be looked at in detail, and various problems posed. How have certain animals become stranded? What affect does the current have on the animals? Are more animals washed up after a spring tide than after a neap tide? What special adaptation do, (*a*) seaweeds, (*b*) seashore animals, have so that they can normally resist these forces? How do these seashore creatures feed? Movement of species can be investigated. Reproduction (necessity for fish to lay large numbers of eggs): effects of high tide on the coastline: erosion and accretion. The dependence of animals on the sea for food, etc.

References

LISSEN, E. F., *Beetles of the British Isles* (London: Warne & Co., 1959, 2 Vols.).

ROSS-CRAIG, S., *Drawings of British Plants* (London: Bell, 1948—1967), unfinished).

WODENHOUSE, R. D., *Pollen Grains; their Structure, Identification and Significance* (New York: Hafner Publishing Co., 1959).